SEWING
BASICS

SEWING BASICS

WENDY GARDINER

BARRON'S

A QUARTO BOOK

First edition for the United States, its territories and dependencies and Canada, published in 2003 by Barron's Educational Series, Inc.

All inquiries should be addressed to:
Barron's Educational Series, Inc.
250 Wireless Boulevard
Hauppauge, New York 11788
http://www.barronseduc.com

International Standard Book No. 0–7641–5596–2

Library of Congress Catalog Card No. 2002116522

22.⁹⁵

Conceived, designed, and produced by
Quarto Publishing plc
The Old Brewery
6 Blundell Street
London N7 9BH

QUAR.SEBA

Project Editor: Fiona Robertson
Art Editor: Anna Knight
Designer: Tanya Devonshire-Jones
Illustrator: Kate Simunek
Editor: Mary Senechal
Assistant Art Director: Penny Cobb
Photographers: Martin Norris, Paul Forrester
Proofreader and Indexer: Pamela Ellis

Art Director: Moira Clinch
Publisher: Piers Spence

Manufactured by
Universal Graphics Pte Ltd, Singapore

Printed in Singapore
by Star Standard Industries Pte Ltd

9 8 7 6 5 4 3 2 1

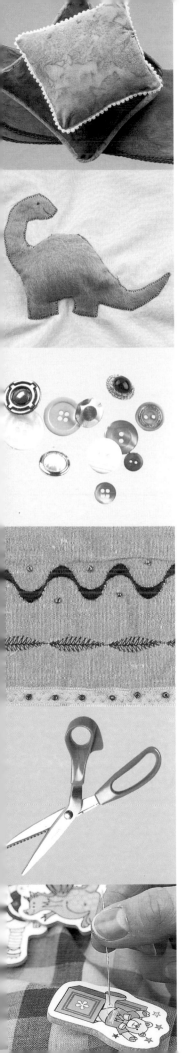

CONTENTS

INTRODUCTION

Sewing is a great hobby as well as a practical skill that allows you to create clothes and furnishings exactly as you like them and at a fraction of what they'd cost in a store. Once you have mastered the basic techniques described in this book, you will be able to tackle any project

with confidence—and I can assure you that the first time someone asks, "Where did you get that great outfit?" and you reply, "I made it myself," you will be hooked!

My aim in this book is to take you step by step through everything you need to know about sewing. I have begun with a comprehensive section on getting started, which includes an explanation of how to choose a sewing machine to suit your budget and growing expertise. I've listed features that I feel are "must-haves" on a sewing machine because they make life so much easier—such as snap-on feet, stitch speed control, an easy buttonhole function, and the ability to stitch a wide range of fabrics. I hope that once you have read this section you will consider your sewing machine a friend and asset rather than something to be wary of! Similarly, my list of essential equipment includes all those handy tools that make sewing easier and quicker, from seam rippers to vanishing marker pens. I've also included a chapter on hand sewing. While most of today's sewers work with machines, there are still occasions when hand

> "SEWING IS A SKILL THAT ALLOWS YOU TO CREATE CLOTHES AND FURNISHINGS EXACTLY AS YOU LIKE THEM AND AT A FRACTION OF WHAT THEY'D COST IN A STORE."

stitching is necessary, and so I cover the basic stitches such as running stitch, backstitch, and gathering stitch.

The Techniques and Projects section explains all the techniques you need to start sewing like a professional—moving from simple straight stitching to making buttonholes, inserting zippers, and adding facings, waistbands, collars,

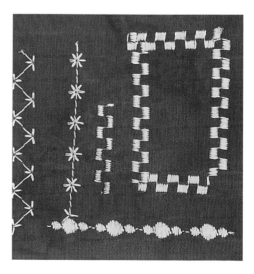

and cuffs. To help you master the techniques, each explanation is followed by a project that allows you to use your new skills right from the start. The projects are simple at first and then become more complicated as you acquire new skills—progressing from a useful drawstring bag and stylish cushion covers to a set of airy window curtains and a kimono that you could make in different sizes for the whole family.

I've also included a glossary to demystify sewing terms so that the next time you hear words like "with nap," "notches," "selvages," or even "stitch in the ditch," you'll know what they mean! In addition, there's a comprehensive troubleshooting guide to explain how and why things occasionally go wrong and to help you rectify the problem.

Sewing is a rewarding pastime and one with limitless possibilities. When you sew, you are not just making things to wear or decorate your home, you are creating works of art, using threads as paints, fabric as canvas, and a sewing machine as your brush! I've been sewing since I was a young child and still find it endlessly enthralling. I hope that with this book as your companion, you too will "get the bug" and go on to enjoy a lifetime of sewing.

Wendy Gardiner

"THE FIRST TIME SOMEONE ASKS, 'WHERE DID YOU GET THAT GREAT OUTFIT?' AND YOU REPLY, 'I MADE IT MYSELF,' YOU WILL BE HOOKED!"

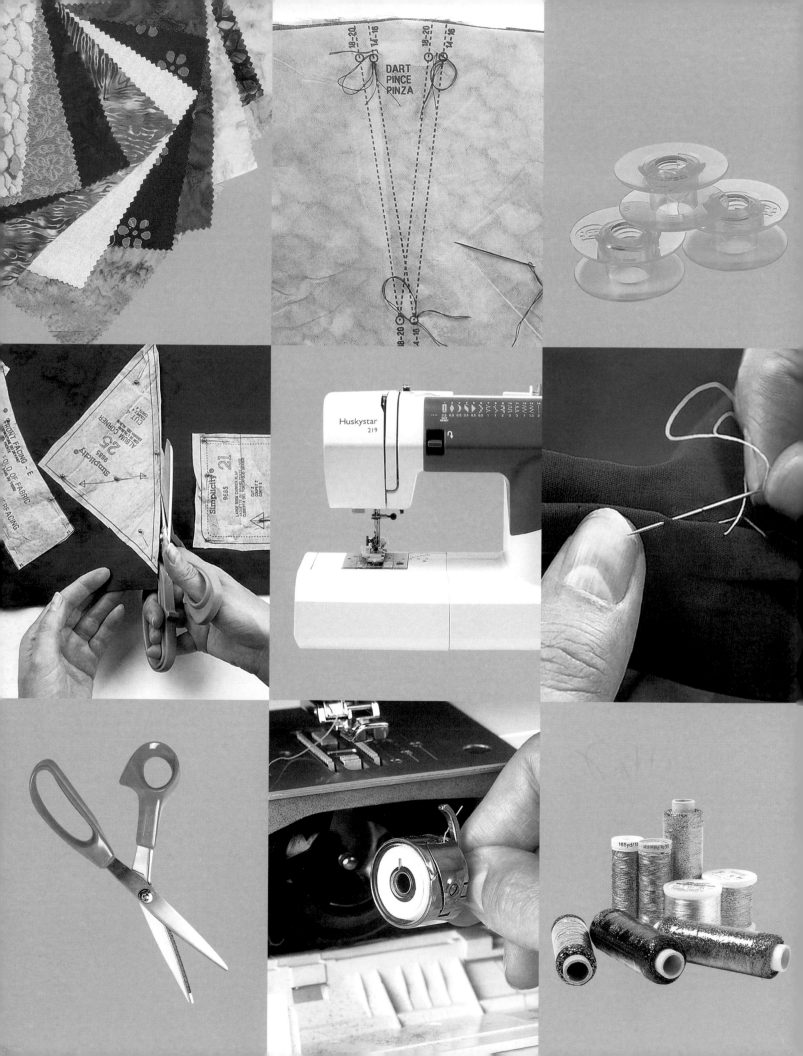

GETTING STARTED

The best way to approach any new project is to make sure you have everything you need on hand before you start. I've therefore begun this book by looking closely at all the equipment and hand-stitching techniques that will make machine sewing simpler, quicker, and a real pleasure to do. Choosing suitable thread, interfacing, and fabric, and working with the right needles, scissors, and sewing machine, will make it all the easier for you to start sewing professional looking projects for your home and family.

MATERIALS

THREAD

Originally, thread was made of cotton, linen, or silk, but today these fibers are often mixed with nylon, polyester, rayon, or viscose to produce stronger, more versatile threads that match the extensive range of fabrics now available.

A good-quality thread is essential when sewing—use inexpensive brands for basting only. Poor-quality threads are often made from uneven fibers, resulting in rough thread that breaks easily.

CHOOSING THREAD

◄ Select a thread with a similar fiber content to that of your chosen fabric. For example, a wool crepe needs a natural fiber thread, such as a 100 percent cotton; silk crepe de Chine sews best with a special silk thread; and polyester voiles need a 100 percent polyester thread, or a polyester-covered cotton. "Universal" threads are good for all-purpose sewing and dressmaking.

Matching the fiber content of fabric and thread is not the only consideration. Fabrics with stretch—knitted fabrics, for example—must be sewn with thread that "gives" correspondingly. The 100 percent polyester threads and the polyester-covered cottons are suitable, because they provide the elasticity that will be needed in the seam when the garment stretches.

SILK THREAD

Silk thread, which has a high luster, is a luxurious and expensive alternative to all-purpose threads for stitching silk and silk-mix fabrics. It is perfect for hand sewing, because it is gentle on the hands.

METALLIC THREAD

► Metallic threads are generally used for decorative stitching, by hand or machine. They make embroidery shimmer and turn simple top stitching into a decorative feature. To avoid the thread snagging or breaking, use it with a needle designed for the purpose, or a large-eyed needle with a sharp point.

TIP: *If the thread is uneven or bulky, use it on the bobbin instead of threading it through the top. Sew with the project wrong side up, so that when it is turned over, the special thread is on the right side.*

MACHINE EMBROIDERY THREAD

▶ Machine embroidery thread is slightly finer than regular sewing thread, because an embroidered design often requires a high concentration of stitching in a small area. There is a large choice of machine embroidery threads available, including metallic, iridescent, variegated, and high luster threads. As with other threads, some are 100 percent cotton while others are a mixture of cotton/viscose or cotton/polyester.

BOBBIN THREAD

Use bobbin thread (also known as bobbin fill) in the bobbin when machine embroidering. It is designed to reduce bulk in the concentrated stitching areas and it produces soft, even embroidery. Available in black or white, bobbin thread is strong and fine and will not show through to the right side.

TIP: *Use a machine embroidery needle to prevent threads from splitting or breaking.*

◀ SPECIAL-PURPOSE THREAD

Some less frequently used threads are suitable for specific purposes:

Quilting Designed for hand or machine quilting, these threads are 100 percent cotton or a polyester/cotton mixture. They are fine and strong, with a wax finish to prevent tangling.

Basting Intended for hand basting and tailor's tacks, basting thread is fine 100 percent cotton that breaks easily but does not tangle or knot.

Top stitch Used for sewing buttons, top stitching, decorative sewing, and hand sewing, this thread is usually thick, strong polyester. Use a regular thread in the bobbin.

Transparent/invisible This thread is designed for hand or machine use in making repairs, quilting, and attaching trims. It is made of nylon, in smoke color or clear only.

SERGING THREAD

▶ Sergers (see page 25) need a large quantity of thread to form the stitches. Special serging threads are fine and strong, and are supplied on larger spools and cones.

100 percent spun polyester is used in the needle threader. The looper threads are either bulked threads (also known as woolly nylon to machine knitters) or floss. The bulked threads give a matte finish and the floss a shiny decorative edge. The bulked threads are especially suitable for stretch and knitted fabrics because they give good coverage on knitted edges. They also make an attractive contrast edging.

TIPS FOR BUYING THREAD

• *To color match thread and fabric, unwind the thread and place a strand across the fabric. Choose a darker shade if a perfect match is not available.*

• *Buy all the thread color needed at the same time. Most garments require two spools.*

• *Keep a store of basic colors, such as black, white, cream, red, navy, green, yellow, and brown.*

INTERFACING

Interfacing is the material that provides support, stability, and control to dress, furnishing, and craft fabrics. It helps the fall, silhouette, and shaping of the finished item.

Most interfacings are nonwoven, lightweight, washable, and do not wrinkle. They can be cut out economically because they have no grain line. Interfacings are available in white or charcoal, in sew-in or fusible (iron-on) varieties, and are sold in packs or by the yard.

TIP: *When using fusible interfacing, always test it on a fabric scrap. Follow the manufacturer's instructions for using steam and a press cloth.*

INTERFACINGS FOR CRAFTS AND INTERIOR FURNISHINGS

These include interfacings with volume, to add body and bulk to projects.

Batting This is used to add padding or to give a soft feel to garments or furnishings. Some battings have pre-printed quilting lines, others are fusible or high in bulk. Those with extra "loft" (compressed fleece to add bulk) are used for items such as quilts and padded wall hangings. There is also a heat-resistant batting (again with compressed fleece) that is useful for projects requiring this protective dimension.

Extra-heavy, sew-in This gives maximum stiffness to tiebacks for drapes, to backings for wall hangings, and to other craft projects.

Preprinted, iron-on, extra-firm valances and tiebacks These are very heavyweight, preprinted backing interfacings, with a choice of valance or tieback shapes.

INTERFACINGS FOR DRESSMAKING AND CRAFTS

IRON-ON FUSIBLES

Fusible interfacings give speedy results, but use them only on fabrics that are suitable for hot ironing and steam pressing.

Super-light, iron-on This is a fine, soft interfacing for lightweight, delicate fabrics, such as rayon/viscose, silks, sheers, and cottons.

Easy-fuse, ultra-soft This comes in three weights: light, for delicate fabrics, cottons, polyester, and soft jacket weights; medium, for gabardine, wool crepe, and linens; and heavy, to provide a structured look in suitings, coatings, and heavyweight cotton blends.

Standard iron-on This comes in two weights, both suitable for cottons and cotton blends. The weights provide different effects: medium gives the fabric a crisp feel, and firm lends a stiff finish.

SEW-IN

Always use sew-in interfacings with special fabrics, such as those with beads or sequins; with pile fabrics, such as velvets and furs; and with fabrics that require a cool iron.

Three weights are available: light, for delicate fabrics, such as those with surface interest or nap; medium, for heavier-weight fabrics, including velvets and furs; and heavy, for wool gabardine, tweeds, coat fabrics, and crafts.

TIPS FOR APPLYING INTERFACING

• *As a general rule, select an interfacing that is lighter in weight than your fabric (unless making items such as valances).*
• *Use sew-in interfacing on fabrics such as velvet, metallics, or corduroy—where pressing fusible interfacing could damage the outer fabric—and on sheer, delicate silks and silk-like fabrics.*
• *Trim away any interfacing in the seam allowance, to reduce bulk. This also makes ironing easier.*
• *When using fusibles, press carefully with a hot iron and press cloth. Lift the iron between pressings.*
• *Always wait for fused pieces to cool completely before handling them. This helps the adhesive to stick firmly.*

SPECIAL INTERFACINGS

Some interfacings, such as edge tape, ease tape, bias tape, and waistbanding, are designed to provide support in specific areas.

▶ **Stitched, reinforced interfacing** This is a soft fusible interfacing with close-set warp threads to give stability. It is good for tailoring, and is suitable for use on both natural and synthetic fabrics.

Edge tape Approximately ¾ in. (2 cm) wide, this fusible tape comes on a roll and is used for stabilizing weak areas or preventing unnecessary stretching at armholes, necklines, lapel breaks, and so on. Bias tape is similar, but cut on the bias and reinforced with a row of stitching. It is used on curved areas or on fabrics cut on the bias, to prevent too much stretch.

Perforated tape This is a lightweight, single, perforated fusible tape, which gives an accurate straight edge to hems, cuffs, and pockets.

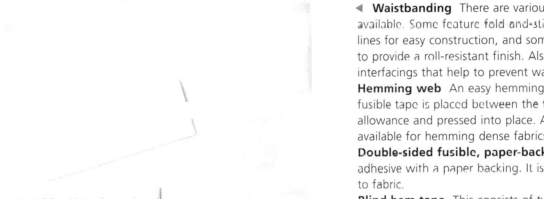

◀ **Waistbanding** There are various fusible waistband products available. Some feature fold-and-stitch lines or perforated fold lines for easy construction, and some include an additional tape to provide a roll-resistant finish. Also available are firm, sewn-in interfacings that help to prevent waistbands from wrinkling.

Hemming web An easy hemming option, this double-sided fusible tape is placed between the folds of the fabric and hem allowance and pressed into place. An extra-strong version is available for hemming dense fabrics, such as denim.

Double-sided fusible, paper-backed This is a web of soft adhesive with a paper backing. It is used to appliqué fabric to fabric.

Blind hem tape This consists of two 1¼-in. (3-cm) wide strips of lightweight, iron on fusible interfacing, stitched together, with the adhesive on the outside. It is good for blind hems on skirts, pants, and jackets, and especially effective on curtains, nets, sheers, and voiles.

STABILIZERS

▶ **Tearaway, sew-in stabilizer** This is used to back machine embroidery, giving stability and preventing the stitching from puckering or being drawn into the feed dogs. Once stitched, the excess is torn away. It can be tricky to tear out of intricately stitched areas.

Self-adhesive embroidery backer This is used for small areas, such as pockets, collars, hats, and handkerchiefs. It is helpful for distortion-free machine or hand embroidery.

Soluble This is a fine, sometimes plastic-looking fabric that is used when machine embroidering. Once stitched, the fabric is washed under running cold water to remove the stabilizer. Wash gently and briefly and the fabric retains some stiffness. Wash completely and it becomes soft to handle.

FABRIC

Which fabric to use when? What are grain lines, selvages, bias, and nap? Here are the answers to most questions—and tips on sewing special fabrics.

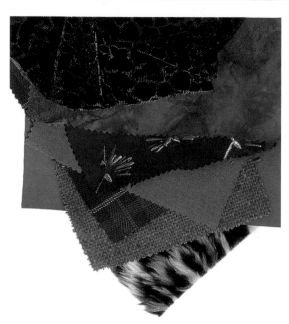

FABRIC TYPES

There is a multitude of fabric types from which to choose. The best-known are grouped here, with hints on how to handle them.

COTTONS AND LINENS

◄ Probably the easiest fabrics to sew, cottons and linens are stable, can range from lightweight to heavyweight, and have every conceivable application. Use fusible or sew-in interfacing in a weight that matches the weight of the fabric and stitch with all-purpose thread. Finish seams by overcasting with a zigzag stitch or by using pinking shears (see Basic seam finishing, page 43). These fabrics can be pressed with a hot iron.

Cotton, polyester/cotton Lightweight, suitable for craft projects and summer clothing, cotton fabrics are easy to sew, come in a huge variety of colors, and are easily laundered.

Egyptian cotton, lawn, gingham These are lightweight cottons with specific uses. Egyptian cotton makes excellent sheeting. Gingham—a two-tone check—can be used for dressmaking or crafts. Cotton lawn is crisp but lightweight, and is often used for lining bridal wear or for other traditional work such as christening gowns or linen tablecloths.

Linen, handkerchief linen, linen-like Linen fabrics wrinkle easily—it is their identifying feature. Treat them the same way as cottons.

Drill, canvas Heavier-weight cottons for outdoor or hardwearing items.

SILKY FABRICS

▼ These include silks, satins, crepe de Chine, polyester, viscose, and rayon. Silky fabrics can range from lightweight to heavyweight. Both sew-in and fusible interfacings are suitable. Seam finishing is necessary because these fabrics usually unravel. Overcast or bind seam allowances with fine binding tape. Iron on the silk setting and use a press cloth.

Silk, silk noil, raw silk, silk crepe de Chine Raw and nubbed silks have uneven surfaces and shading. Treat as a pile fabric and use the "with nap" cutting layout (see With nap, page 17) provided with the pattern.

Satin, satin-backed crepe A high-sheen fabric, satin is medium in weight and perfect for evening wear. Use the "with nap" layout to be sure of even shading. Satin-backed crepe can be used on either side, and is good for evening suits.

Polyester, viscose, rayon, polyester crepe de Chine
These synthetic fabrics mimic the appearance and feel of natural fibers but are often less expensive and easier to sew. They will unravel easily, so seam edges must be finished. Use lightweight interfacing, either sew-in or fusible, to match the fabric.

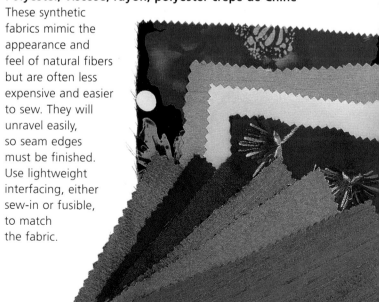

WOOLEN/FLEECE FABRICS

▼ There is a great variety of woolen fabrics, ranging from lightweight wools to heavy meltons and tweeds. Lightweight wools are suitable for blouses and dresses, and the heavier weights are used for coats and jackets. If the fabric has a sheen (cashmere, for example), use a "with nap" layout. Press with care, using a press cloth.

Wool crepe, challis, georgette, gabardine These are lightweight fabrics that can be used for general dressmaking—skirts, dresses, pants, and suits. Easy to sew, they have minimum stretch if pattern pieces are correctly placed on grain lines. Fusible or sew-in interfacing is suitable.

Cashmere, melton, mohair Use the "with nap" layout. Test press a scrap first to check whether this flattens the pile—place a fluffy towel over the fabric, if necessary. Trim pile from seam allowances. Bulk can also be reduced by grading the seam allowances (see Trimming and grading, page 42) and by using a lining fabric for facings.

Fleece A pleasure to work with, fleece comes in many colors and designs, doesn't need seam finishing, washes easily, and can be used for many outerwear garments and accessories, or furnishings. Press with care, however, because a hot iron leaves marks. Use a slightly larger than usual seam allowance to help feed fabric layers evenly—but trim close to stitching to reduce bulk in seams.

Tweed, worsteds, corduroy, bouclés In addition to usually being heavyweight, these can also have a nap and a directional weave, so choose the "with nap" layout. Use lining fabric for facings to reduce bulk. Finish seams with overcasting.

TIP: *If fabric sticks as it is fed through, and a special foot is unavailable, sprinkle talcum powder along the stitching line.*

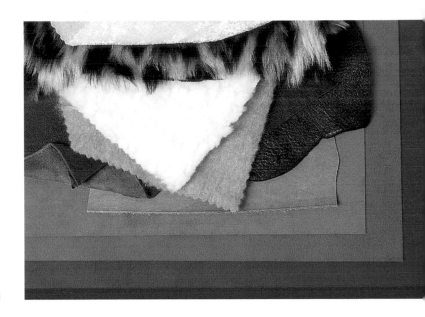

PILE FABRICS

▲ Avoid pressing with steam, which may flatten the pile. Use a velvet board or a soft towel as a pressing surface. Choose "with nap" layouts and sew-in interfacings.

Velvets: panne, chiffon, velveteen, sculptured, devoré
Velvets are luxury pile fabrics that can be synthetic, cotton, or silk, and can be floating and lightweight or heavyweight. A devoré velvet has parts of the pile burned away to leave a raised pattern. Velvet can be difficult to sew because the piles rub together, causing them to "walk" when seams are stitched. Avoid this by double pin basting and thread basting, and using a walking foot. Cut all garment pieces with the nap running in the same direction. Decrease bulk in seams by grading seam allowances. Finish seams by overcasting or binding with fine binding tape.

Fur Fur fabrics can have pile that ranges from close cut to long and shaggy. Fake furs do not unravel, so the seams do not need to be finished. Reduce bulk in the seams by trimming away fur pile from the seam allowances. Using a sturdy pin, and working from the right side, pick out the fur along the seams to cover and disguise the seaming.

Synthetic leathers/suedes These include faux suede, ultra suede, suedette, leatherette, and pleather. Synthetic leathers and suedes rarely need finishing, so seam allowances can be trimmed close to stitching. Reduce bulk by grading the seams.

Use weights or tape when cutting. If pins are needed, use them only in the seam allowance, because they may make holes in the fabric. If the presser foot sticks to the leather, use a roller foot or a foot with a nonstick coating.

LUXURY FABRICS

▶ Most luxury fabrics should be treated as if they have a nap, and cut out following "with nap" layouts. Use sharp scissors and change needles frequently, since they will blunt more easily. Use sew-in interfacings, and press with care—always with a press cloth.

Taffeta, chiffon, georgette, organza, voiles Fabrics that shimmer and gently change color through the width or length of the piece are termed iridescent, ombre (shading), or changeant (changeable). When cutting out, check that balance marks and notches are in line across the fabric, so that color variations match. Use lots of pins to secure flimsy fabric, and sharp, serrated shears.

Sequined/beaded fabric These luxury fabrics are often used as part of a garment. Remove beading and sequins from seam allowances by carefully cutting away or crushing. Choose simple designs for highly beaded or sequined fabrics. Cut on a single layer of fabric, turning pieces over to be sure of right and left sides. Use the "with nap" layout to cut all pieces in the same direction. When sewing transparent fabrics, use sew-in interfacings or a layer of matching lining fabric.

Surface detail, pre-pleated, ruched, crushed Do not press fabrics with pre-pressed surface detail, such as crushed velvets, crinkled, and pre-pleated fabrics. Trim seam allowances and bind with fine binding tape. Be sure to match balance marks and notches with the same surface detail on both sides.

TIP: *If the beads are bulky and cause stitching problems, use a zipper foot.*

TIP: *When handling beaded fabrics, apply drafting tape to stop sequins or beads from unraveling at the edges.*

STRETCH FABRICS

◀ These include knits, jerseys, stretch velour, Lycra, and spandex. Use stretch stitches or zigzag stitch to sew seams. Interface with a woven stretch interfacing. Prevent excessive stretching at vulnerable areas, such as armholes and neck edges, by stabilizing with edge tape. Press carefully, with a press cloth. Use a ballpoint needle. Take care when pinning, because snags and runs are easily caused by pins catching the fabric.

CUTTING OUT

Many fabrics can be cut out in double layers or when folded, which makes the cutting process quicker. There are rules to follow, however—and, of course, exceptions to the rules.

▶ **Folded fabric** When cutting on a fold, check that the fabric is folded evenly, right sides together. Most pattern layouts call for fabric to be folded lengthwise, with selvages matching. Pin pattern pieces to the wrong side, matching grain lines (see below).

Selvages These are the side edges of the fabric. They may be slightly more tightly woven than the main fabric, and they don't require finishing when used as an edge.

◀ **Lengthwise or straight grain** This is the direction of the fabric weave that is parallel to the selvages. The lengthwise grain line has least stretch. Place pattern pieces with grain lines marked on them carefully in line with selvages to be sure they are on grain. Fabric cut off grain will have more stretch.

Crosswise grain This is at right angles to the lengthwise grain and follows the threads that run from selvage to selvage. There is slightly more stretch in the crosswise grain.

▶ **Bias and true bias** Bias is any diagonal direction. True bias is found by folding the fabric so that lengthwise and crosswise grains meet. Fabric cut on the bias is at its stretchiest. It is perfect for making bias binding tape. Garment sections cut on the bias may need stay stitching or edge stitching at curved areas, such as necklines.

Single layer Occasionally it is necessary to cut pieces for a single layer of fabric. Work with the fabric right side up. If two pieces are to be cut from one pattern section, remember to place the pattern piece face down for the second cutting to ensure a right and a left piece.

▼ **With nap** This is the term used when laying out fabrics that have a pile, one-way shading, or a design. Pattern pieces are placed so that the pile will run in the same direction on all corresponding pieces. For better wear, position pieces with nap running down (that is, smooth when felt downward).

TIP: *If unsure whether a fabric has a nap, always use the "with nap" layout.*

TIP: *For fabrics that appear to have no right or wrong side, use the side with the raised holes or marks in the selvage as the wrong side, and mark every piece cut out with a pin or chalk.*

Patterned, striped, and checked fabric Cut each piece from a single layer, so that tissue pieces can be placed accurately on the fabric. Check that stripes and checks are squared off, and that wide stripes or checks do not run across the widest part of pattern piece (bust or hips). When cutting the second pattern piece, match up balance marks and notches, so that seamed pieces will have an unbroken pattern.

PINNING

Attach pattern and fabric layers securely before cutting out to be sure of accurate results. Use pins, pattern weights, or even food cans to keep them in place. For slippery or pile fabrics, insert pins close together. For cottons and other stable woven fabrics, pins can be more widely spaced.

TRANSFERRING BALANCE AND PLACEMENT MARKS/NOTCHES

Cut out around notches, not into the seam allowance. Transfer all placement and balance marks to the wrong side of the fabric pieces immediately. Remove pins to avoid unnecessary pin marking.

TIP: *Avoid stripes and checks until confident with pattern matching. Use simple designs.*

TIPS: *.An allover pattern (a pattern that covers the whole fabric and works in the same way in all directions) is perfect for novice sewers, because the pattern design will hide any imperfect stitching.*

ESSENTIAL EQUIPMENT

MACHINE AND HAND NEEDLES

There is a range of machine and hand needles to choose from. Change your needle according to the type of fabric and thread you are using.

HAND NEEDLES

▶ Keep a packet of mixed household needles for general hand sewing and for taking thread ends through to the back of the work after machine stitching. Mixed packs contain a variety of needle sizes, sometimes with different eye sizes also. Replace these and all needles and pins regularly, because blunt needles can snag fabrics.

In addition to household needles, there are special needles for embroidery, beading, furnishings such as curtains and rugs, and so on. Beading needles are very fine, curved, and small-eyed, so that they slip through bead centers easily. Upholstery needles are often sturdy, with big eyes to take thicker threads or cording. Some are also curved, which helps when it is impossible to reach the back and front of the work—when finishing sofa covers, for example.

TIPS FOR USING MACHINE NEEDLES

- *Keep a selection of different-sized needles on hand.*
- *As a general rule, heavy fabrics require thick needles; fine fabrics need fine, sharp needles.*
- *Replace needles after every project.*
- *If a needle breaks easily, try a larger size.*
- *If stitches skip or seams draw up as you stitch, try a smaller needle.*

SERGERS

Sergers (see page 25) need different needles, which are available in a choice of sizes and finishes. Check your serger manual for details on which to use and when.

TIP: *Make needle threading easier by cutting thread at an angle.*

MACHINE NEEDLES

▼ Universal, or multipurpose, machine needles are suitable for regular machine sewing. These are available in sizes to suit the fabric and thread being stitched. American sizes range from 9–20 and European sizes from 60–120 (see Needle sizes, page 124). Needle packets are usually numbered with the relevant size—the larger the number, the larger/stronger the needle. In addition, there are needles for specific purposes, such as sewing denim or silk, and doing embroidery or decorative stitching.

Universal/multipurpose This is used for most woven, synthetic, and knitted fabrics.

Ballpoint The rounded tip separates the fibers instead of piercing them, making this needle good for fabrics such as knits, velvets, and fleece.

Stretch This needle has a specially designed "scarf" to help stitch two-way stretch fabrics, such as those containing Lycra or rubber, which are used for lingerie and swimwear. This needle will help prevent skipped stitches.

Jeans A sharply pointed needle, often with a blue top, this is designed for denim, canvas, and other tightly woven and heavy-duty fabrics. It is also excellent for top stitching heavy fabrics.

Leather This needle has a chisel point to help it penetrate real leather. For ultra-suede or faux suede, use a jeans needle.

Sharps Also known as a microfiber needle, this is sharply pointed and suitable for sewing silks, microfiber, and densely woven fabrics. It is also good for top stitching and buttonholes.

Embroidery Use this larger-eyed needle when stitching with special threads, metallics, and rayons, or when machine embroidering.

Twin This is two needles grouped in one shank to use for top stitching and decorative heirloom stitching. The gap between the needles can vary from approximately 1/16–1/8 in. (2–3 mm). Twin needles are also available as ballpoint, universal, stretch, and embroidery needles.

Quilting This needle usually has a long, sharp point, designed to pierce layers of cotton or batting while maintaining a straight stitch.

CUTTING TOOLS

Different tasks need different tools. Apart from regular household scissors, there is a range of cutting tools to make your sewing tasks easier and more effective.

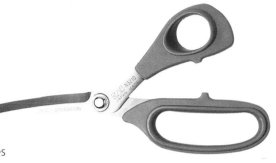

SHEARS

▶ The most important cutting tool for a sewing project is a pair of shears. They can be right- or left-handed, and have bigger handles than scissors, with a larger hole for the fingers than for the thumb.

The long blades of shears enable dressmakers to cut seams quickly, with a long, smooth action and the fewest possible cuts. Most shears have an angle between handle and blades that keeps them—and the fabric—flat on the table during each cut.

Shears with serrated blades are useful for cutting fine fabrics. The serrated teeth hold the fabric in place as you cut, which is excellent when dealing with slippery fabrics, such as satins and silks.

PINKING SHEARS

▶ Available with a soft or hard grip, pinking shears have zigzag-notched blades that provide the "pinked," or saw-toothed, cut. They provide a speedy way of finishing raw edges, especially on cottons and other non-fray fabrics, and craft projects.

AUXILIARY CUTTING TOOLS

SHARPENERS

▶ Scissors sharpeners help keep blades sharp and free from nicks. Do not sharpen serrated blades, however, because this would damage the edges.

ROTARY CUTTERS

▶ Rotary cutters are terrific for cutting long bias strips (for bias binding) and for cutting patchwork fabrics. They are used in conjunction with a cutting mat and ruler and can cut several layers in one sweep. Look for those with retractable blades and/or those with changeable blades for different cutting effects.

SEAM RIPPER

▶ The seam ripper—also known in Europe as a quick-unpick—is a handy item that is usually supplied among the sewing-machine tools. It has one sharp end, a curved blade at the base, and usually a bead on the top arm. It is used to undo incorrectly stitched seams and may also be used for cutting through buttonholes.

SCISSORS

Scissors can be used in the right or left hand and have blades of equal length. Scissors with soft-touch handles provide a gentler grip. There are also scissors with handles that are gripped in the whole hand, instead of with fingers and thumb; a spring action between the blades opens them gently between each cut.

NEEDLEWORK SCISSORS

▶ Small embroidery, needlework, or short-blade scissors are the perfect companion to shears. The small-sized blades provide much greater control for intricate cutting, and are useful, therefore, for notches, clipping curves, or trimming seam allowances close to stitching.

QUICK CLIPS

▶ These are a handy tool for snipping thread ends and cutting or snipping small sections of fabric. They are palm-held and have very short blades, which enable you to keep close to the work area and snip threads at seam ends quickly and easily.

SPECIAL SCISSORS

▶ Scissors for special purposes include appliqué, buttonhole, and machine embroidery scissors. Appliqué scissors have a shield to hold the fabric flat as you cut. Buttonhole scissors can be adjusted to a specific size of cut. Embroidery scissors have sharp, fine points, and are often curved at the tips to help snip threads close to stitching. They are especially useful for cutting thread ends on machine embroidery work.

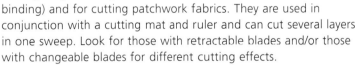

MARKING TOOLS

Marking pattern pieces saves time when matching piece to piece, and makes fitting, pocket placement, and darts easier to complete.

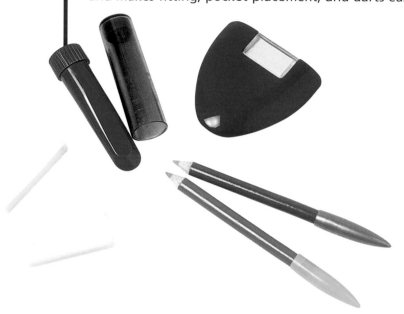

The key to a good fit is to construct with accuracy. This is easy to achieve when placement points, sections to be joined, dart width and length, buttonhole positions, and so on, are marked on the corresponding fabric pieces. The placement marks are usually indicated on the tissue of printed patterns, and just need to be transferred to the fabric—usually on the wrong side.

There is a range of marking tools available and it is a good idea to keep a selection in your sewing kit so that you can use the appropriate method for each job. If fabric is especially bulky, fine, or textural, making pen and chalk marks difficult to see, the best option may be to stitch marks in the traditional way, using tailor's tacks (see page 31) rather than a marking tool.

CHALK

Chalk is a great way to mark accurately, and it disappears when brushed. Chalk markers come in many shapes and colors—from the traditional tailor's triangle of chalk to chalk wheels and chalk pencils tipped with plastic brushes. Chalk wheels make a fine powder line, and are useful for marking long lines, such as those for pleats and darts. Chalk triangles and pencils can be used in the same way as regular pencils to mark lines, crosses, dots, and so on. Use a color that contrasts with the fabric, and mark on the wrong side of the fabric.

1 Push a pin through the tissue paper and fabric layers at the marking dots and, lifting the tissue carefully, mark the placement position on the first side.

2 Turn the layers over with care, and mark the reverse piece at the pin point. Repeat for all placement points.

MARKER PENS

▶ Pens are handled in the same way as chalk pencils. They can be water-soluble, "fadeaway," or permanent. Pens are convenient to use, but they should not be applied to dry-clean only fabrics or delicate materials, such as silks.

Water-soluble pens are usually blue, and the mark can be removed with a damp sponge or by washing the garment. "Fadeaway" pens—sometimes known as evaporating or air-soluble pens—are usually purple, and their markings dissolve within 48 hours. "Vanishing" pencils are also available and work in the same way as "fadeaway" pens.

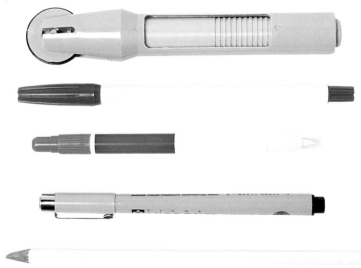

TRACE TACKING

▶ This is a row of basting stitches (see Basting, page 30) along placement lines, which is used when marking the position of items such as pockets. Use a chalk pen or pencil first to transfer placement dots to the wrong side of each fabric piece. Remove the tissue and, using contrasting colored thread, sew large basting stitches along the placement lines.

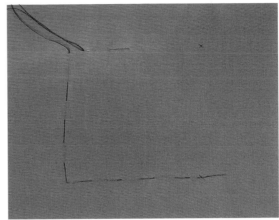

PRESS MARKING

This method is suitable for tucks and pleats, or for other straight edges with fold lines. It is done on the ironing board, and pins can be pushed into the board to secure the items as they are pressed.

1 With tissue in place, clip the ends of the fold line within the seam/hem allowance.

2 ◀ Remove the tissue. Fold the line in place from clip to clip, pinning into the board, if necessary. Press.

TRACING PAPER WHEEL

Dressmaker's carbon paper (also known as dressmaker's tracing paper) can be used with a tracing paper wheel to apply line markings to both sides of the fabric simultaneously. However, this method is not suitable for textured or bulky fabrics, on which the markings could be hard to see. Old-style carbon paper produced a permanent mark and was therefore unsuitable for use on the right side or on delicate fabrics. Modern carbon paper is made in a variety of colors and can be sponged off with clear water. Use a color that is close to the fabric color. As with any ink-based markings, mark on the wrong side of the fabric.

1 Remove the tissue paper and set it to one side; then turn the fabric pieces so that the wrong sides are together.

2 Slip a piece of folded carbon paper between the layers, with the carbon sides toward the fabric. Replace the tissue paper and repin in position.

3 ▶ Using a ruler as a guide, run a tracing wheel over the markings to be transferred. Mark dots with an X, so that one line of the X follows the stitching line.

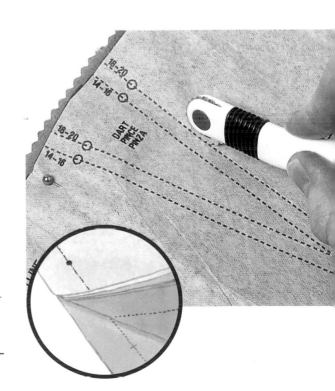

TIP: *Always test pen or carbon paper markings by applying them to a scrap of fabric and then ironing it. Even "fadeaway" and carbon paper markings may remain if pressed with a hot iron.*

THE SEWING MACHINE

A sewing machine is an essential tool for anyone wishing to sew garments or interior furnishings easily, quickly, and with professional-looking results.

Your sewing machine stitches fabric layers together by interlocking two threads, creating a lock stitch with an upper thread (coming through the needle) and a bottom thread (coming from the bobbin). The length and tension of the stitch determine how well the stitches are formed on different fabric weights and numbers of layers. If the tension is correct, the top thread will show on the top of the fabric and the bottom thread on the underneath. The threads interlock between the layers.

Sewing machine parts

Sewing machines vary, but the general principles remain the same from model to model. Check your manual for details on the position of the relevant features on your machine.

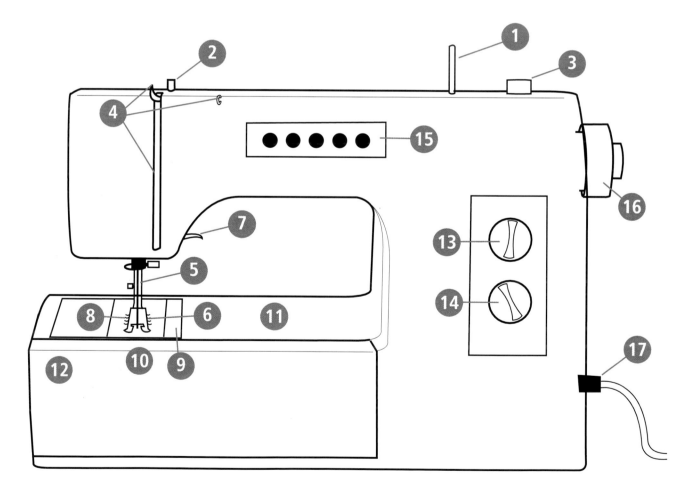

1 Thread spindle/spool pin This holds the thread spool.

2 Thread tension guide Controls the upper thread and helps form stitches correctly (the average tension setting is often highlighted).

3 Bobbin winding disk Used when winding bobbins—see your sewing machine manual for threading guidelines.

4 Upper thread guides These may be color-coded. Follow the manual for threading procedure.

5 Needle This is held in place by a screw. Most machines offer a choice of needle positions—center, right, or left.

6 Presser foot Used to hold fabric flat as it is fed through the machine.

7 Presser foot lever Used to lower and raise the presser foot.

8 Feed dogs Help guide the fabric through as it is stitched. If the feed dogs are lowered, the fabric can be self-guided for free machine embroidery.

9 Throat plate (or needle plate) Fits over the feed dogs and usually has markings to indicate seam allowance distances from the needle position. The needle goes down through the throat plate opening to meet the bobbin thread and form the stitches.

10 Bobbin case and bobbin The bobbin is either dropped into the case, or the case is removed and the bobbin inserted vertically into it. Bobbins are wound on the bobbin winder (check the manual for instructions).

11 Free arm Most machines convert from flat bed to free arm by removing the extension table.

12 Flatbed extension table This clips on and off the free arm, and often contains an accessory box.

13 Stitch length This depends on the fabric and the type of stitching. It can be altered, step by step, using a dial or button (older machines may use a lever with a screw mechanism), between a preset minimum and maximum stitch length.

14 Stitch width This can be increased or decreased for stitching zigzag or decorative stitches.

15 Stitch selection Turn a dial or press a button to indicate the selected stitch. Most machines alter the tension automatically.

16 Flywheel Used to raise and lower the needle slowly. On some machines, an inner disk deactivates the needle when winding the bobbin.

17 Sockets These are provided for the foot pedal and power cord.

GENERAL THREADING GUIDE

UPPER THREAD

Incorrectly threading the upper thread is a leading cause of thread breakage and skipped or too tight stitches. Follow the diagram in your manual carefully. The thread comes off the spindle, then goes around some retainers, through the tension disks (check that it's between these), up and over a moving holder, down to the needle, and through to the back.

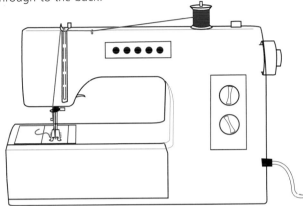

Hook race bobbin insertion

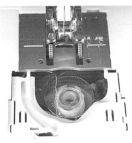

Drop-in bobbin

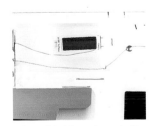

Thread held on the spindle with a restrainer

BOBBINS

Wind bobbins with the bobbin winder so that the thread feeds evenly. If it is wound unevenly or too loosely, the bobbin can jam. Most machines come with several bobbins. For general sewing, use the same thread in the needle and the bobbin. When sewing with special threads, use a regular or bobbin-fill thread in the bobbin.

The bobbin thread is wrapped around the bobbin case, as indicated in your manual. To bring up the bobbin thread, turn the flywheel slowly to lower the needle, which will catch the bobbin thread. As the upper thread comes back up, pull it gently from the back to bring up the bobbin thread loop. Pull both together a short way.

TIP: *Hold both threads at the back when taking the first stitch to prevent them, or the fabric edge, from being pulled down into the throat plate.*

CHOOSING AND ADJUSTING STITCHES

▶ Most machines have a choice of "utility," or preprogrammed, stitches. These are basic stitches used in general sewing and include straight stitch, zigzag, stretch stitch, and blind hem stitch. To use these for different sewing techniques, the length and width can be altered—for example, a zigzag stitch can be used to overcast a raw edge, or as a tight satin stitch for buttonholes or appliqué.

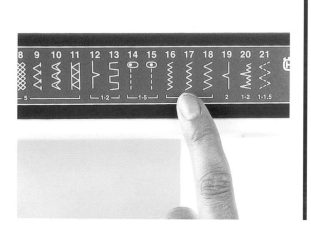

TIP: *Always test stitch alterations on scraps of main fabric, with interfacing and any other components, to check that they work correctly. Keep adjusting the length or width until you are satisfied with the stitch formation.*

All-purpose foot

Buttonhole foot

Embroidery/ appliqué foot

Blind-hem foot

Zipper foot

WHEN PROBLEMS OCCUR

As the machine stitches, fabric fluff (lint) builds up in the bobbin area. If this is not routinely cleared, it can cause bobbin jams. Remove the bobbin and defluff it regularly, with the help of the little cleaning brush supplied with your machine.

If the top thread spool keeps bouncing up and down the spindle, the thread can tangle or break. Prevent this by adding a spool cap to the spindle, which keeps the thread in place. One or two caps are usually supplied with the machine.

Most modern machines are self-lubricating, but check the user manual and oil as indicated, if required. (For more troubleshooting hints, see pages 122–123.)

PRESSER FEET

▲ ▶ Presser feet hold the fabric in place while it is being sewn. Every machine comes with a range of sewing machine feet for the basic sewing functions. Using the correct foot for the task at hand makes sewing much easier.

All-purpose foot This is used for most straight stitching. It usually has two equal-length toes and an oblong gap through which the needle penetrates.

Buttonhole foot Most modern machines have special feet for buttonholes. Some measure the button and automatically stitch the correctly sized hole. The underside has deeper grooves to allow it to glide over satin stitching.

Embroidery/appliqué foot Often made of transparent plastic, this foot has a high, wide groove on the underside to help it glide over decorative stitching.

Zipper foot This allows stitching close to the bulk of the zipper teeth. It may have a central toe with the needle penetrating either side or a choice of snap-on positions to move the foot from side to side.

Blind-hem foot This usually has a wide toe to the right, with a guide, and a narrow toe to the left.

BUYING A SEWING MACHINE

KEY FEATURES

There is a huge variety of machines to choose from, with prices ranging from hundreds to thousands of dollars. Which you choose will depend on personal preference. However, it is essential to check a few basic features:

Capability to sew all types of fabric Your machine should be able to handle everything from fine voiles and chiffons to heavy brocades, velvets, or layers of denim. Most modern machines have a variable foot pressure, which allows them to stitch different weights easily.

Variable stitch speed This is especially useful for sewing around curves and corners, and when adding appliqué.

Snap-on feet These can be readily changed and allow you to use the appropriate foot for each job.

Easy-to-thread bobbin and needle Being able to wind the bobbin without unthreading the needle is a useful feature if the thread runs out mid-seam.

Wide table/additional extension table This is useful if you intend to sew larger items, such as curtains.

Electronics/foot control Check the machine's guarantee for restrictions in these areas.

Portability If you need to move your sewing machine around, check the weight and the carrying case for portability.

Accessories Are there accessories you can add to your machine at a later date? Not essential but handy, for example, is a buttonhole foot—slip the button in the back, and the machine will sew a correctly sized buttonhole every time.

TIP: *Check out a range of machines—take your own fabric samples to the store and test drive different machines to see which handles them best.*

◄ *Drop the feed dogs if you want to apply some free-motion embroidery.*

SERGERS

◄ Sergers (also known as overlockers) stitch seams, and trim and finish them at the same time. A simple serger has three threads, but there can be as many as eight. The stitches are flexible, which is useful for stretch fabrics, such as sportswear. These stitches are created very quickly and lend a professional, ready-to-wear finish to garments.

The stitches are formed by a combination of upper and lower loopers and needle threads. Sergers use far more thread than a conventional machine, so serger thread is finer and supplied on much larger spools, or cones. Each of the needle threads and loopers has its own thread tension. Needles and feet perform the same function as on a sewing machine, but can rarely be interchanged between the two types of machine.

The cutting blades, to the right of the needle, cut off excess fabric as it is sewn. These can usually be disengaged when using the serger for decorative stitching. Use a serger alone or as a complement to a conventional sewing machine.

PRINTED PATTERNS

There are many international pattern companies, such as Burda, Butterick, Kwik Sew, McCalls, New Look, Simplicity, and Vogue. They use similar pattern markings and terminology, and produce multisize patterns, so that several sizes are available in one package. The pattern pieces are printed on tissue paper, accompanied by step-by-step instruction sheets, and supplied inside an envelope that illustrates the designs included and gives details of requirements.

TIP: *For tops, jackets, and dresses, use your bust measurement to determine pattern size. For skirts and pants, use your hip or fullest part measurement.*

PATTERN SIZING

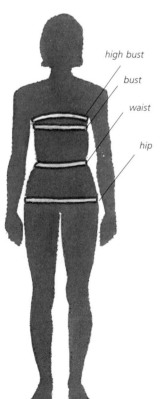

high bust

bust

waist

hip

Pattern sizes are not the same as ready-to-wear sizes, so you must take accurate measurements before you can determine your pattern size. You may also need different sizes for top and bottom.

◄ The basic measurements that determine pattern size are:

High bust Measure directly under the arms, above the bust, and around the back. The tape should fit snugly but not tightly.

Bust Measure around the fullest part of the bust. The tape should remain parallel with the floor.

Waist To find the natural waistline, tie a string around the waist, and bend the body from side to side. The string will roll into the crease that forms at the natural waistline.

Hips Measure at the fullest part—approximately 8 in. (20 cm) below the waist. If the stomach is the fullest part, measure there instead.

► Commercial printed patterns are sized for different body types. The average woman is categorized under the heading "Misses," at a height of 5 ft. 5 in.–5 ft. 6 in. (165–168 cm). Misses' patterns are generally made for a B cup with a 2½ in. (6 cm) difference between the bust and high-bust measurements.

Fuller and/or taller figures are categorized as "Women" or "Women Plus," and most pattern companies also produce Junior/Teen sizes. Children's patterns are sized by age and average measurements.

Misses   *Women*   *Junior*

FIT AND EASE ALLOWANCE

A common problem experienced when making patterns is that the finished size is either bigger or smaller than expected. This is often due to the amount of wearing and design ease allowance built into the pattern, which, in turn, depends on whether it was designed to be close fitting, fitted, semi-fitted, or loose fitting. The wearing ease is the amount of "wiggle" room needed—a close-fitting bodice has very little, whereas a loose shirt has a lot more. The design ease is a fashion feature: the extra fullness that the designer builds in to create the desired silhouette.

The total amount of ease also depends on the garment type—a greater wearing ease allowance is made for coats than for blouses, for example. As a guideline, the following allowances are frequently used:

Knit fit A very close fit; the garment measures at or under the body measurement.
Close fit A very close fit; 1/8–1/4-in. (3–6-mm) ease.
Fitted The garment contours closely to the body; 1/2–1 1/4-in. (13–31-mm) ease.
Semi-fitted The garment skims the figure, following the body shape; 1 1/2–2-in. (4–5-cm) ease.
Relaxed/loose fit An "easy" fit, with 5 1/2–7-in. (14–18-cm) allowance for tops, and 4–5 1/2-in. (10–14-cm) allowance for skirts and pants.
Very loose fit Best described as oversized, the garment is very loosely fitted with ample room inside.

TIP: *Compare the finished garment measurements, printed on the pattern envelope or pattern tissue, with your body measurements to calculate the amount of ease allowed.*

THE PATTERN ENVELOPE

The front of the pattern envelope shows the design and design variations supplied, by means of photographs and/or line drawings. The back lists a host of useful information, for example:

Size range This indicates the sizes included in the pattern and the measurements for each size.
Back views These are small line drawings of the back, and sometimes the front, of the designs. They show zipper placement, pleating, necklines, and so on, which may be obscured in the photograph.
Garment details Another indication of the design detail, this states whether the item is close or loose fitting, the type of closure (such as a zipper), whether there is lining, and so on.
Notions Details of all the items required to complete each design are listed, including the length of zipper or number of buttons, and the type of interfacing needed.
Fabric requirements The type of fabric suitable for the designs and the amount required are given. The list of suitable fabrics includes those in which the pattern has been tested. If plaids, checks, or stripes are suitable, this is stated. If it is not, avoid them, because fabric matching would be difficult.

The amount of fabric needed to make each garment is indicated in each size. There will be amounts listed for "with nap" and "without nap," as well as the amounts needed for different fabric widths. When only one amount of fabric is listed for each size, the width of fabric is generally 45 in. (115 cm), so you need to allow a little more if your chosen fabric is 36 in. (90 cm), or less if it is 60 in. (150 cm). Most pattern catalogs have a fabric width conversion chart to help with this calculation (or see the chart on page 124).

Finished garment measurements This information helps you to judge whether the garment will be too short, too long, or very loose fitting. If the measurements are not on the envelope, they will be on the pattern tissue pieces.

fabric cutting layout for a pair of pants

selvages

fold line

PATTERN TISSUES

Pattern piece Each tissue sheet has several pattern pieces printed on it. Each piece is marked with a number, the name of the piece (sleeve, front, or collar, for example), the number of pieces to be cut, and so on.

◄ **Multisize cutting lines** Multisize patterns show several sizes on each pattern piece, indicated by bold lines. Sizes are sometimes differentiated by variations in marking, such as dotted or dot-and-dash lines. These bold lines are the cutting lines. The advantage of multisize patterns is that you can smoothly cut from one size to another. For example, you might want to cut a size 14 top but a size 12 hip.

Although the seam allowance is included in most manufacturers' patterns, it is not shown on the tissue of multisize patterns because the number of lines needed would be confusing. Dressmaking patterns include, on average, a ⅝-in. (15-mm) seam allowance. Other types of pattern include a ¼-in. (6-mm) allowance. The seam allowance provides a margin for sizing and fit.

Notches Notches are small triangular markings found on the outer edges of pattern pieces. They are used to match pieces together at the front and back, and at the sleeve and the armhole. Cut them outward—not into the seam allowance.

Circular marks These indicate the placement of features such as darts, pockets, zippers, facings, and so on. To transfer them to the fabric pieces, use a marking tool (see pages 20–21) or tailor's tacks (see page 31).

Grain line This is shown on the tissue by a thick straight line with directional arrows at either end and is especially important in dressmaking patterns. Matching the straight grain line with the grain line of the fabric ensures that the garment hangs properly and does not droop, twist, or pucker. The grain line of the fabric is parallel to the selvage.

◄ **Fold line** Some pattern pieces can be placed on the fold of the fabric, so that two halves are cut at once. This is indicated by a squared-off grain line arrow. This line is placed against the fold of fabric (with the fabric folded so that the selvages match).

► **Lengthening/shortening** Some patterns can be easily lengthened or shortened to suit individual needs. Simply cutting off the bottom or adding to the length, however, would alter the design line. The lengthening/shortening points are placed so that the alteration will not spoil the finished line. Details about how to make the adjustments are provided on the instruction sheet in the pattern package.

▼ **Tucks, pleats, and buttonhole placement** These are shown by dotted or dashed lines. Pleats and tucks may also have directional arrows between the lines indicating which way to fold the fabric to form the pleat.

notches

multisize cutting lines

circular marks

grain line

fold line

lengthening/shortening lines

INSTRUCTION SHEET

The instruction sheet provides more than the step-by-step instructions for making the pattern. Also included are:

Line drawings These show all the pattern pieces in the package, each with a separate number or letter. Each design lists the pieces that are needed.

▲ **Fabric layouts** These show the best way to lay out the fabric depending on the size being cut and the fabric width, and whether the fabric is "with nap" (all pieces must be laid in the same direction on "with nap" layouts). They also indicate whether to cut from single or double layers of fabric.

General directions This section explains pattern markings, describes how to cut, mark, and make adjustments, and gives other general advice.

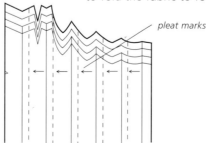

pleat marks

TIP: *Highlight the layout you are following when putting the tissue onto the fabric to make sure you keep to the same one.*

BASIC TECHNIQUES

CUTTING PATTERNS

Using a pattern as a template makes it easier to cut out fabric accurately, especially when more than one piece of the same size and shape is needed.

◀ Make a pattern by drawing around an object with a simple shape, or use patterns from magazines or pattern companies (see Printed patterns, pages 26–28). Whichever pattern you use, positions for buttons, zippers, motifs, or pieces to be joined must be marked on the pattern and transferred to the fabric.

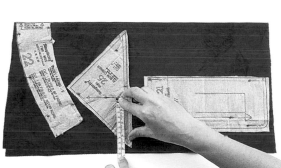

FOLD LINE ▶

If a pattern piece is symmetrical, it can be cut on a fold of fabric, which saves time. Fold fabric with right sides together, matching selvages at sides. Position the pattern piece on the fold as indicated by the marking.

GRAIN LINE ▶

Probably the most important marking on a dressmaking pattern is the grain line, which indicates how the pattern piece must be placed on the fabric. The grain line on the pattern must run parallel with the selvage or grain of the fabric. When working with two or more layers at a time, pin through all layers at either end of the grain line, making sure that the distance between the grain line and the selvage is the same. Then pin the pattern piece around the edges through all layers.

CUTTING OUT

1 Use sharp, paper-cutting scissors to cut out the pattern. For speed, the paper pattern need only be cut roughly at this stage.

2 Once the pattern is pinned to the fabric, check the layout. If using a "with nap" (see page 17) layout, are all the pieces laid in the same direction? Do they follow grain lines or are they on fold lines or single layers, if necessary? Will patterns, stripes, or checks match on joined seams? To ensure that they do, make sure notches that go together are placed on the same part of the check, stripe, or pattern.

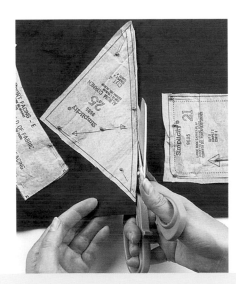

3 ◀ Use dressmaker's shears to cut out the piece, cutting accurately around the pattern through all layers.

4 Transfer markings from the pattern to the fabric, using your chosen method, and remove the pins.

TIPS: *Cut out around the notches using small embroidery scissors for greater accuracy.*

For easy reference, keep pattern pieces folded with the fabric pieces until you are ready to use them.

CUT TWO

Patterns published in magazines or supplied by pattern makers indicate how many of the same pieces are required. If making your own pattern, record this information to remind you of what is needed.

SEAM ALLOWANCES

Seam allowances are needed to allow some flexibility and to provide an edge to finish in order to prevent the fabric from unraveling. Allowances average $1/4–5/8$ in. (6–15 mm). Once a seam is sewn, the seam allowance is trimmed, clipped, and finished by pinking, overcasting, or binding (see Seam finishing, page 43).

MARKINGS

Mark on the pattern any placement lines that must be transferred from the pattern to the fabric. This ensures that they are positioned correctly and, if repeated on a second project, made identical each time. (See Tailor's tacks, page 31, and Marking tools, pages 20–21, for more information about marking methods.)

BASTING

Basting, or tacking, is used to hold two or more layers of fabric together temporarily before stitching. There are two methods of basting: pin and stitch.

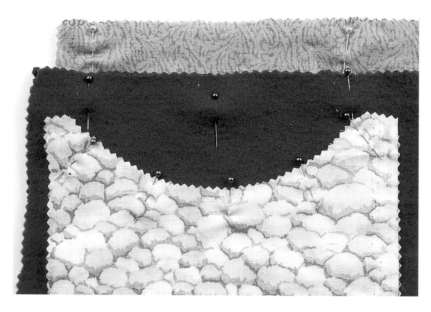

PIN BASTING

This quick method is useful for attaching simple pieces. Place the pins at right angles to the edges for easy removal when machine stitching.

1 For straight seams in a lightweight or medium-weight fabric, pin baste every 6 in. (15 cm).

2 Reduce the gap between pins to 2 in. (5 cm) at curved or gathered areas or on slippery fabrics.

3 For heavier fabrics, such as fleeces and woolens, pin every 3–4 in. (8–10 cm).

TIP: *Use glass- or plastic-head pins, which are easier to remove quickly—and to see if dropped!*

THREAD BASTING

Thread basting is especially useful when securing trickier areas—such as sleeves in armholes, collars, pleats, and zippers—and when a garment is tried on for fit before the final stitching.

1 Use a double length of thread in a contrasting color, and start at one end with a large knot.

2 ▼ Make large (³⁄₈-in./1-cm) running stitches along the stitching line (see Running stitch, page 32).

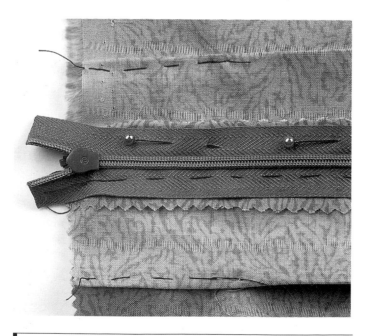

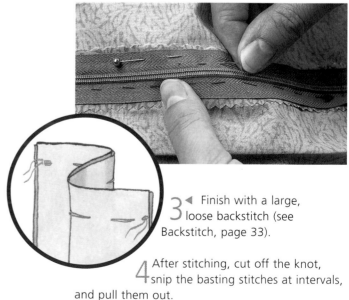

3 ◄ Finish with a large, loose backstitch (see Backstitch, page 33).

4 After stitching, cut off the knot, snip the basting stitches at intervals, and pull them out.

TIP: *When basting pale fabrics, use a light contrasting color and baste just inside the seam allowance to prevent color staining.*

TAILOR'S TACKS

Tailor's tacks are used to transfer pattern markings to the fabric pieces—especially for pocket, zipper, and dart placement. They are also particularly useful for very bulky, fine, or textural fabrics where chalk or pen marks would be difficult to see. Pin the pattern tissue to the fabric layers first. Use a long piece of double thread, knotted at the end, in a bright contrasting color that will show up for easy removal.

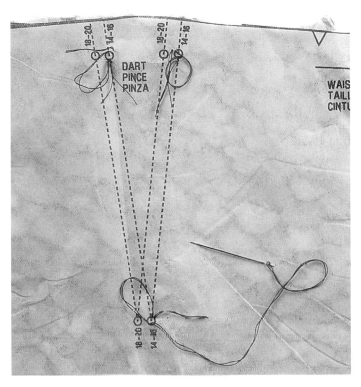

1 ▶ Begin at the first pattern dot symbol, stitching through the pattern and layers of fabric. Work from front to back and up to the front again, leaving a slight loop on the underside.

2 ◀ Repeat, making a scant $\frac{1}{8}$-in. (3-mm) stitch and leaving a loop on top and bottom.

3 Cut threads, leaving a 2-in. (5-cm) thread tail. Repeat for all markings.

4 ▲ Snip thread loops on top, taking care not to pull on the thread, then gently lift the pattern away.

5 ▶ Carefully separate fabric layers and snip threads between them, so that some thread remains in each layer.

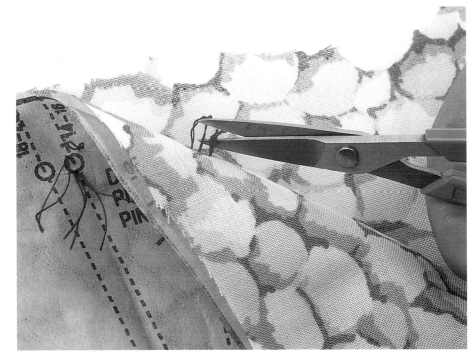

HAND STITCHING

Today, hand sewing is used mainly to repair garments, to alter hems, or to finish off a machine-stitched project. A few basic stitches, therefore, are adequate for most occasions.

Depending on its purpose, hand stitching can be done using a single or a double strand of all-purpose thread. Special threads that are thicker and stronger can be used for topstitching and buttonholes, where necessary, and for more heavy-duty sewing.

FIRST AND LAST STITCH

Repeated backstitch on the spot, or a loop caught by the first or last stitch, can be used to secure the thread at the beginning or end of a seam.

BACKSTITCH ON THE SPOT

◀ Push a threaded needle through the material from back to front, and pull up until just a small ½-in. (13-mm) tail remains. Hold this tail with one thumb while pushing the needle back through the fabric at the same spot as before, two or three times, making a few backstitches on the spot.

LOOPED THREAD

If using a double strand of thread, thread the needle with the loop end and pull through to leave tails at the top. Make the first stitch through to the back and up again to the front, slipping the needle through the loop before pulling tight.

Having secured the thread, you can now stitch the seam with one of the following three stitches.

RUNNING STITCH

This is a small, even row of stitches that is used in delicate sewing where the stitches will be permanent.

1 ◀ Take the threaded needle through to the back, then bring it up through to the right side again, approximately ⅛–¼ in. (3–6 mm) in front. Pull all the way through. Repeat along the length of the seam.

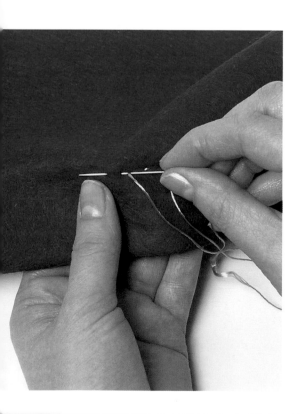

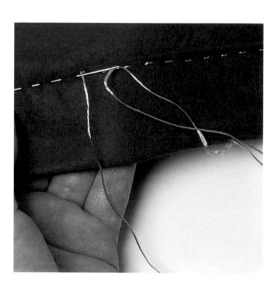

TIP: *Draw the seam line with a chalk marker or vanishing marker pen, so that you have a straight line to follow.*

2 ▲ Running stitches can be done in groups of 3–4 at a time, as above, making this a quick stitch to complete.

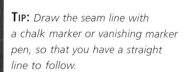

BACKSTITCH

This stitch is the closest hand stitch to machine stitching.

1◄ Having secured the thread at one end, as above, push the needle through from the right side to the back and up again to the right side, approximately ⅛ in. (3–5 mm) in front.

2 Next, put the needle back through the fabric at the point of the first insertion, and bring it through to the right side approximately ⅛ in. (3–5 mm) farther along. Repeat along the entire seam, making sure that each stitch is positioned next to the other.

3◄ If you check on the reverse side, you will see that the stitches overlap slightly.

GATHERING STITCH

Similar to a running stitch, a gathering stitch is used literally to gather an edge. For a long edge, always use doubled thread for extra strength. Do not gather more than 20 in. (50 cm) at a time. For greater lengths, start a new row of stitches, with a knot at the beginning, to continue the line.

1► Double knot one end of the thread and pull the threaded needle through from back to front. Take up 3–4 long running stitches at a time. Each stitch can be approximately ⅜–⅝ in. (10–15 mm) long.

2◄ When the width to be gathered is stitched, leave a trailing thread and gently pull up the required amount of gathering.

3◄ To secure stitching and keep gathering in place, backstitch two or three times on the same spot. Cut off the end of the thread.

BLIND HEMMING

Blind hemming is probably the most useful hand stitch of all, since it is particularly good for repairing or taking up hems. Sewing machines may offer the option of blind hemming, using a special foot, but it is often just as easy to do this by hand. (For blind hemming with machine-finished hems, see Blind-stitched hems, page 76.)

1 Turn the raw hem edge to the wrong side by a scant ¼ in. (6 mm) and press. Turn the hem up again from ½–3 in. (13 mm–8 cm), depending on the item being stitched—lightweight fabrics can have smaller hems, weightier wools or curtains need wider hems. Press again.

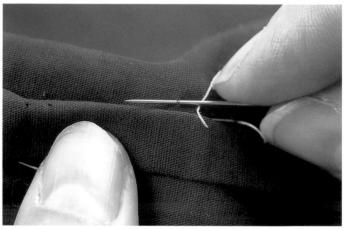

2 Working from the wrong side, pin the folded hem in place, a little way from the actual edge.

3 ▲ Secure the thread at one side seam, as usual. Gently roll back the top of the folded edge and hold it in place with your thumb while carefully catching a single thread from the main fabric.

4 ◄ At the same time, pull the needle through the rolled-down hem edge. You can be more generous with the amount of fabric you catch, since this is the inside of the garment and will not show.

5 Continue along the hem, rolling back the hem edge before catching a single strand of the main fabric each time.

TIP: *The key to achieving a blind hem is to make sure you only catch a single strand of fabric from the main material.*

TIP: ▶ *A great hemming tip for beginners is to use edge tape in the hem allowance to make a perfect invisible hem. Turn up the hem as in step 1 above, then fold back the main hem allowance and press iron-on tape along the length of the hem area. Continue to blind hem stitch as above, but catch the edge tape instead of the main fabric. This guarantees that no stitching will show through to the right side.*

▶ *Careful blind stitching will not show on the right side.*

SLIP STITCH

Slip stitch is virtually invisible and is used to secure hems to linings, attach trims, and close turning gaps left in casings, cushion covers, and so on.

1 ▶ Having secured the thread at one end, as above, slip the needle into the fold of the hem allowance (or underside of trim or one folded edge) and take up a scant 1–3 fabric fibers of the lining or main fabric.

2 ◀ Bring the needle up through the folded hem fabric (or underside of trim or first folded edge), slightly at an angle and in front of last stitch. Repeat along the length to be stitched.

BLANKET STITCH

As well as holding two layers together, a blanket stitch forms a decorative edge. It can be stitched in a coordinating thread or in a contrasting color to create a striking finish. A blanket stitch is best done in a heavyweight thread or fine wool.

1 ▶ Having secured the thread to the side edge of the work, start with the needle at the back. Pull the needle slightly through to the front.

2 ▼ Loop the thread that is attached to the back of the work over the needle.

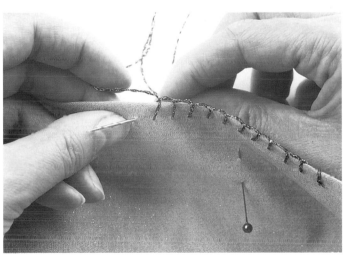

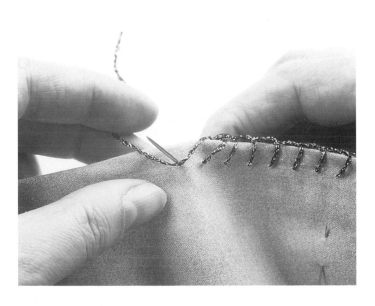

3 Holding the loop in place with one thumb, pull the needle completely through. Repeat, pulling the needle through to the right side from the back again, approximately 1/8 in. (3–5 mm) in front of the previous stitch. Continue to the end of the row. Fasten off with 2–3 backstitches.

TECHNIQUES AND PROJECTS

This section explains all the basic sewing techniques you need to create wonderful items for your home and wardrobe. The explanation of each technique is followed by a project to help you practice your new skills. Starting with basics and progressing to more complex patterns, you'll make a useful drawstring bag, a stylish pillow cover, fun dressing-up clothes for the kids, a sarong, a set of pretty window curtains, and more. Once you've worked your way through this section, you'll be sewing like a professional—making buttonholes, putting in zippers and waistbands, and adding bias binding and trimmings.

STRAIGHT STITCHING

Most seams are joined with straight stitching, so with a little variation in stitch length, you can use it to sew soft furnishings, fashions, and crafts. Learn to machine with straight stitches and you can sew almost anything!

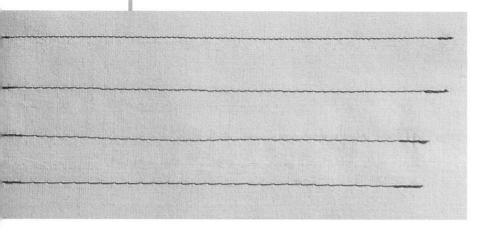

STITCH LENGTH

◄ The length of the individual stitch will differ according to the thickness of the fabric and the number of layers joined. As a general rule, the thinner the fabric, the smaller the stitch can be; and the thicker the fabric or the greater the number of layers, the longer the stitch must be.

Stitch length can be adjusted by pushing a button or moving a lever or dial to the required setting. Some machines have numbers corresponding to the stitch length; others indicate the actual stitch length in millimeters or the number of stitches per inch. Your manual will show which system your machine uses.

Other reasons to adjust stitch length include basting (use a longer length for easy removal), corner reinforcement (at pocket edges, for example), and easing or gathering (see page 40).

STITCH LENGTH GUIDE

Very lightweight chiffon/voiles/muslins:
Set stitch length between 10–12 stitches per in. or 2–2.5 mm.

General sewing, including lightweight cottons, polycottons, georgettes, and so on:
Set stitch length between 8–10 stitches per in. or 2.5–3 mm.

Medium-weight gabardine, wools, worsteds:
Set stitch length between 7–10 stitches per in. or 3–3.5 mm.

Heavyweight wools, fleeces, tweeds, meltons, and so on:
Set stitch length between 5–8 stitches per in. or 3.5–6 mm, depending on the number of layers being sewn.

TIP: *Always test stitch length on a scrap of the fabric to be sewn, using the same number of layers and interfacing.*

GETTING STARTED

▶ Using one hand, pull both the needle and bobbin threads to the back. Place the fabric under the presser foot so that the right edge is aligned to the appropriate marking/distance from the needle to give the seam allowance desired (see Seam allowances, page 42). Lower the presser foot, lower the needle, and begin stitching slowly, holding the thread tails, until at least 1 in. (25 mm) is stitched. Feed the fabric evenly by resting one hand on the front of the fabric to guide it through and the other hand at the back to keep it moving smoothly.

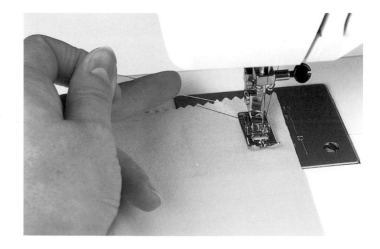

TENSION

In addition to altering the length of the stitch to suit the fabric, it is occasionally necessary to alter the tension. Together, the correct tension and stitch length form perfectly even stitches in which only the top thread shows on the top and only the bobbin thread shows on the underside. To adjust the tension, refer to your sewing machine manual.

GETTING IT RIGHT

- If the bobbin thread shows on the top, the tension is too tight and must be tweaked very slightly to loosen.
- If the top thread loops through to the underside, the tension is too loose and must be tweaked very slightly to tighten.
- For other stitching problems, turn to Troubleshooting (pages 122–123).

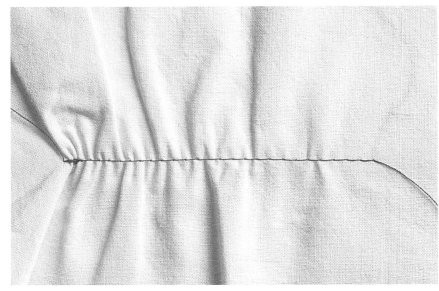

▲ *Tension too tight*

TIP: *Tighten or loosen tension very gently, a little at a time—a small alteration to tension goes a long way.*

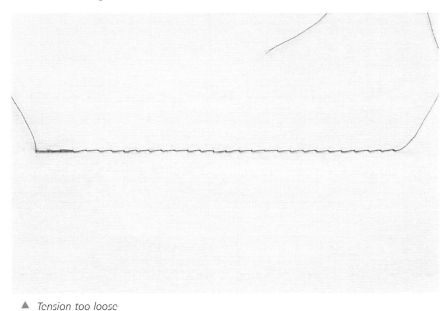

▲ *Tension too loose*

BACKSTITCH

▶ Use backstitches to secure seams at the start and end. Most machines have a backstitch button that you hold in while reverse stitching (on older machines there may be a lever to flip instead).

1 At the beginning of a seam, insert the needle in the seam ½ in. (13 mm) from the end and, holding in the button, backstitch to the edge. Release the button and start stitching forward.

2 Slow down at the end of the seam and, holding in the button, backstitch for ⅜ in. (1 cm) over the last few stitches.

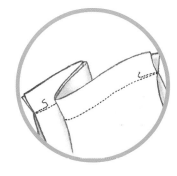

TIP: *If the fabric is pulled down into the throat plate at the start of a seam, use a smaller needle. Alternatively, add a layer of tissue or tear away stabilizer at the start of the seam and remove it later.*

GATHERING

You can use straight stitches to gather lengths of fabric—to fit onto a waistband, for example.

1 Set your machine to the largest stitch possible and stitch in the seam allowance.

2 When gathering lengths of more than 20 in. (50 cm), divide the gather stitching into two or more sections. Stop stitching after 18 in. (46 cm) and leave long thread tails. Start again to complete the row.

3 ▶ Pull the bobbin thread to gather the fabric. Make sure that the other end of the thread doesn't pull through.

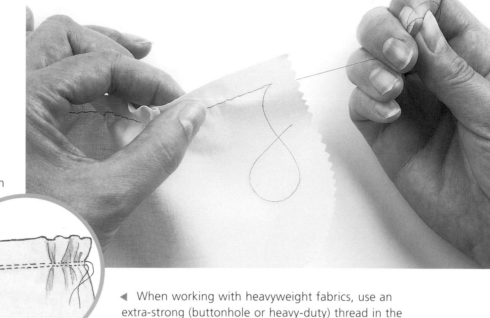

◀ When working with heavyweight fabrics, use an extra-strong (buttonhole or heavy-duty) thread in the bobbin, and stitch two parallel rows of gather stitches. Pull them up together, again using the bobbin thread.

STRAIGHT STITCHING BY OTHER NAMES

Patterns often refer to ease stitching and stay stitching—both of which are straight stitching but used slightly differently for particular purposes. Reinforced stitching is also a variation of straight stitching.

EASE STITCHING

Used to ease a length of fabric onto a shorter length, ease stitching is similar to gathering, but no gathers are visible on the finished item.

1 Loosen the tension slightly and set the stitch length to 8–10 stitches per in. or 2.5–3 mm.

2 Stitch within the seam allowance, close to the seam line, continuing ½ in./13 mm beyond the notches on the pattern. If necessary, stitch a second row parallel to the first, still within the seam allowance.

3 ◀ Pin the eased seam to the adjoining section, matching notches, curves, and so on. Draw up the eased fabric, using the bobbin thread to distribute the fullness evenly.

4 Complete the seam by stitching along the seam line, with the eased side uppermost.

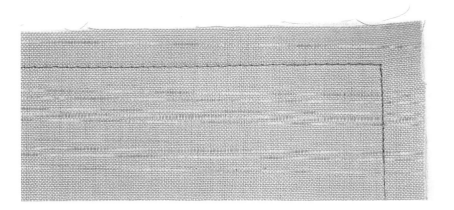

STAY STITCHING

◀ Stay stitching is used to prevent fabric from stretching and is applied to fabrics cut on the bias and curved areas, such as necklines, which stretch more easily than straight edges. This stitching would be done first.

1 ▼ To prevent the fabric from stretching while you stay stitch, sew in the direction of the fabric grain. Find the fabric grain by "stroking the cat." Run your finger along the cut edge, note the direction in which the fibers curl smoothly, and stitch in that direction.

2 Use a regular stitch length and sew close to the seam line—¹/₂ in. (13 mm) from the cut edge.

TIP: *Some patterns print directional arrows for stay stitching—follow these where applicable.*

REINFORCED STITCHING

◀ Reinforced stitching is used to strengthen areas where extra pressure is likely or those areas that are trimmed close to the stitching, such as corners or curves. Reduce the stitch length to 18–20 stitches per in. or 1.5 mm, and stitch 1 in. (25 mm) on either side of the curve or corner, over the seam line.

OPENING A SEAM

▶ Occasionally it is necessary to open a seam. Use the seam ripper accessory supplied with the machine. Insert the blade into stitches every 1 in. (25 mm) or so, and then gently pull the seam apart. Do not be tempted to run the seam ripper between the layers along the seam because you can accidentally cut into the fabric. Pick out all the thread and press the seam with steam (use a press cloth on delicate fabrics) to remove the stitch holes.

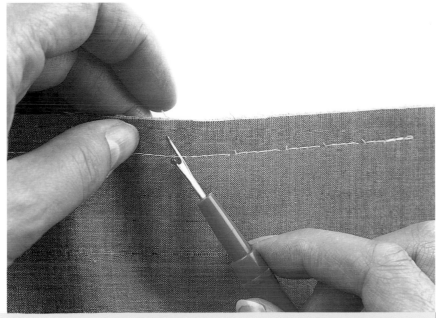

SEAM ALLOWANCES

The seam allowance is the area of fabric between the stitching line and the cut edge. Most purchased patterns include seam allowances of $\frac{5}{8}$ in. (15 mm) on dressmaking patterns and $\frac{1}{4}$ in. (6 mm) on craft patterns. This allows room for handling and adjusting size. Once seams are sewn, most of the seam allowance is trimmed away and the edges finished. Left alone, the fabric can unravel, causing the stitching to fall away.

Add seam allowances to any patterns you create yourself. It is important to keep the stitching lines accurate. For example, a paneled skirt, with three panels in the back and three in front, has six seams. If each is inaccurately sewn by just $\frac{3}{8}$ in. (1 cm), the garment can gain or lose $2\frac{1}{2}$ in. (6 cm) in width.

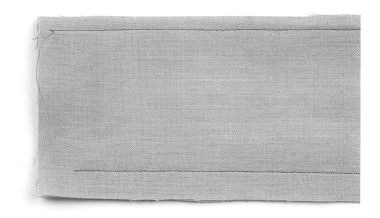

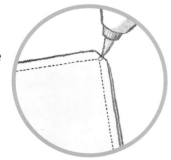

MAINTAINING ACCURACY

There are a number of ways to make sure you stitch accurately.
- ◄ Use the markings on the throat plate—usually indicated in $\frac{1}{8}$-in. (3-mm) increments—or position a piece of tape the distance required from the needle.
- Use the needle position (on most machines this is left, center, or right) measured against the edge of the presser foot.
- Machine or hand baste along the seam line and follow this line when machine stitching. Remove basting stitches afterward. (Use different-colored thread for the basting stitches for easy identification.)
- Mark the seam line with chalk (on the wrong side of the fabric only).

TRIMMING AND GRADING

It is important to trim seams that will be enclosed—sandwiched between two layers—in order to reduce bulk. Enclosed seams are found in collars, cuffs, faced edges, pockets, and so on. Because the seam allowances will be encased, they do not also need finishing.

TRIMMING

▶ Cut the seam allowance to a minimal $\frac{1}{4}$ in. (6 mm). Trim corners at an angle, close to the stitching. If the fabric tends to unravel, dab a spot of fabric glue on the corner stitching.

CLIPPING AND NOTCHING

▶ This technique helps curved areas to lie flat. Inside, or concave, curves simply require little slits or snips in the seam allowance. On outward, or convex, curves, cut wedge-shaped notches from the seam allowance to eliminate excess fabric when the seam is pressed open.

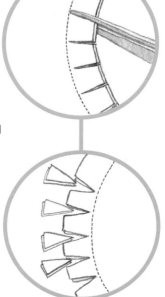

GRADING

◄ Grading is the technique of cutting the two layers of seam allowance at different widths so that the layers do not form a ridge within the encased seam. Trim the seam allowance that will be closest to the inside of the garment to $\frac{1}{8}$ in. (3 mm) and the seam allowance that will lie closest to the outside of the garment to $\frac{1}{4}$ in. (6 mm).

BASIC SEAM FINISHING

For seams that are not encased, the seam allowance needs to be clean finished to prevent unraveling and to provide a professional finish. The most frequently used finishing methods are pinking (on lightweight cottons) and overcasting/overstitching. A third option is to bind the seam allowances—especially useful where the inside of the garment may show.

Overcasting/overstitching

Pinking

PINKING

Using pinking shears, trim seam allowances on both layers together, ¹/₄ in. (6 mm) from the cut edge. Press. With lightweight fabrics, the seam allowances can be pressed together to one side. With heavier weight fabrics, press them open.

OVERCASTING/OVERSTITCHING

Set your sewing machine to overcast stitch or zigzag stitch and, working on the edge of the fabric, stitch the cut edges. Lightweight fabrics can be stitched together but heavier fabrics need each layer stitched separately to prevent bulky seams.

If available, use a serger (overlocker) to finish the seam allowances. Again, layers of lightweight fabric can be stitched/trimmed as one, but layers of heavier fabric should be stitched separately.

BINDING

▶ A bound finish is a very neat way to encase raw edges, and is suitable for any fabric. Use a sheer lightweight tricot seam binding or even bias binding. For best results on fabrics that unravel easily, use a zigzag stitch. On other fabrics, a straight stitch is adequate.

1 To make sure you apply it the right way, tug the binding slightly to see which way it curls. Position the binding over the seam edge so that it curls around the seam allowance.

2 Secure the binding with a pin at the beginning. Once you've stitched the binding a little way, remove the pin and continue stitching, gently stretching the tape so that it encases the fabric edges. As you sew, you will stitch through both layers of tape at once.

For other types of seams and finishes, including decorative seams and those used when working with difficult fabrics, turn to Seam finishes and edges, pages 84–87.

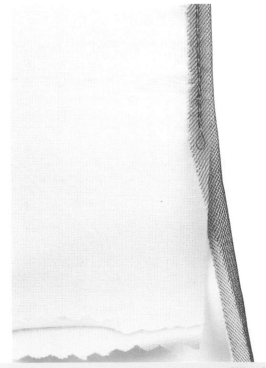

KIT BAG

Stow toys, shoes, and other equipment neatly into these simple bags. Just a few rows of straight stitching and a drawstring—and you're ready to go!

STEP 1 ▼ Cut a panel of fabric, 14 x 36 in. (36 x 92 cm).

TIP: *If working with a striped or a checked fabric (as here), use a straight pattern line as a guide for cutting and stitching.*

STEP 2 ▶ Finish seam allowances of long edges using pinking shears, zigzag stitch, or overlock stitch.

STEP 3 Fold the panel in half, short ends and right sides together. (The folded edge will be the bottom.)

STEP 4 Pin the side edges together, with pins placed at right angles, so that they are easy to remove as you stitch.

STEP 5 ▶ Using a marker pen or chalk pencil, mark the placement of the cord casing three times at the side edges, measuring 2 in. (5 cm), 2¾ in. (7 cm), and 3½ in. (9 cm) down from the top.

STEP 6 ▶ Machine stitch from the fold at the bottom of the bag up to the first marked line. Backstitch/reverse stitch to strengthen, and cut threads. Begin again from the middle marked point and stitch to the top. Repeat on the other side of the bag.

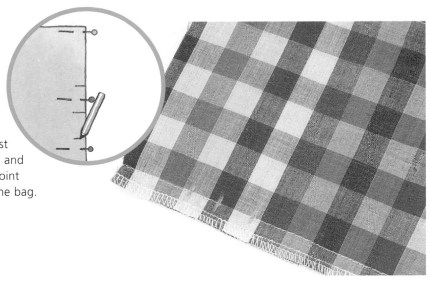

STEP 7 ◀ Press seam allowances open and stitch them down to the main fabric at the casing gap. This will keep them out of the way when inserting the cord later.

STEP 8 ▶ Still working with right sides of the bag together, turn the top over to the wrong side by 2 in. (5 cm) at the first mark. Tuck the raw edge under again, about ¼ in. (6 mm). Press with an iron.

STEP 9 ◀▶ Machine stitch two rows of stitching all the way around, with the first row close to the folded raw edge and the second row ¾ in. (2 cm) from the first (so that the unstitched side edges fall between the two rows of horizontal stitching). Press.

STEP 10 ▼ Cut the cord into two equal lengths. Secure one end and, using the large safety pin as a tool, feed the cord through the casing, around and out at the same side. Repeat, starting at the other side edge. Knot the ends of the cord securely at either side.

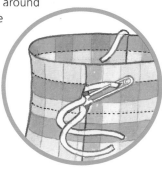

STEP 11 ◀ Add colorful buttons or a motif to denote the bag's contents.

TOP STITCHING

Top stitching is a row of stitches that shows on the outside of a garment, cushion, or curtain. It is done on the outside, usually after seams are sewn—often to add a decorative finish. It can be stitched by hand or machine, using threads that match the fabric or form a bright contrast.

Top stitching can also be used for practical purposes, such as holding facings in place, preventing pocket edges from rolling out, or providing a quick hemming method. In this case, it usually comprises a single row of stitches in a matching color, close to the edge, and is also known as edge stitching.

When top stitching serves as embellishment, just about anything goes! Use brightly contrasting colors; thicker, metallic threads; different sizes and types of stitch; any number of rows of stitching—even add ribbons or trims.

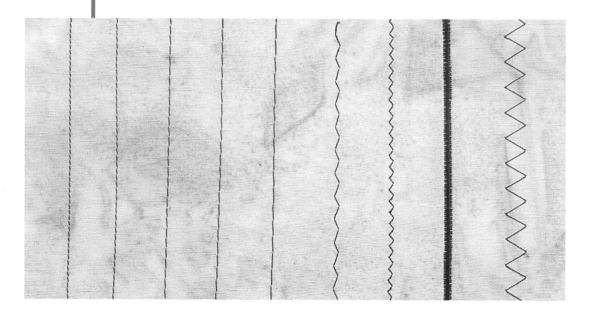

TIP: *When using thicker, textured thread, wind it on the bobbin instead of the top needle and then place the work face down on the throat plate of the sewing machine.*

GETTING STARTED

- Use a slightly longer than normal stitch: 7–9 stitches per in. or 3–3.5 mm.
- Always test stitch a sample piece first. Use the same number of layers of the same fabric and interfacing (if to be used), so that the sample is truly representative. Check out different stitch combinations and lengths.
- Reduce the stitch speed on your machine to control stitching more easily.
- To maintain a straight line of stitching, use a fabric guide along the right edge. You can utilize the edge of the foot, varying the distance between the stitching and the edge by altering the needle position (most machines have at least three positions: left, center, and right).
- Line up the fabric edge with the marking on the throat plate and use this as a guide. If your machine doesn't have markings, stick a length of masking tape on the flat bed, with different distances marked.

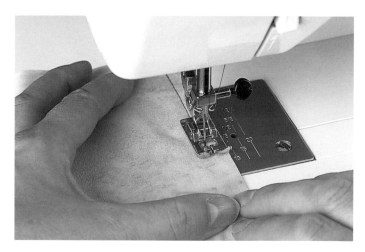

TIP: *Always check that the needle will go through the hole in the foot properly by making a stitch by hand, turning the wheel on the right side of the machine.*

TYPES OF TOP STITCHING

SINGLE ROW OF STITCHING

▶ A single row is the easiest method of top stitching. Stitch ⅛–⅜ in. (3–10 mm) from the edge, using a stitch that is slightly longer than usual.

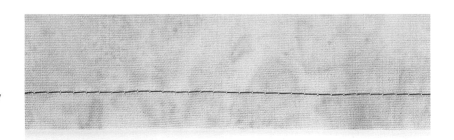

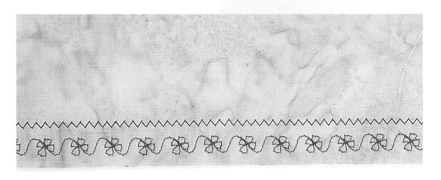

DOUBLE DECORATIVE ROW

◀ Choose straight, zigzag, or other stitches on your machine. Try variations on a test piece first, altering stitch length and distance between rows until you are pleased with the result. Stitch the first row approximately ⅜ in. (10 mm) from the edge of the fabric. Stitch the second and subsequent rows in the same direction as the first.

TWIN ROWS

▶ Use a twin needle to stitch two rows at an equal distance. Vary the look by using different-colored threads in the needles. Add another twin-stitched row of small, closed zigzags. Experiment with the length and width of the stitch to vary the zigzag effect.

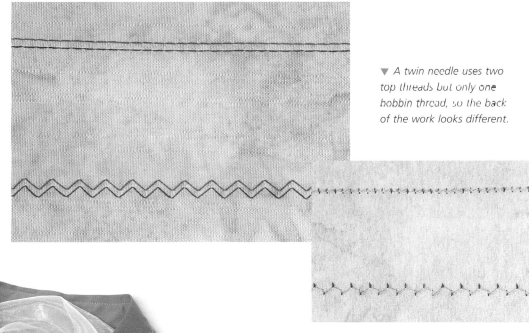

▼ A twin needle uses two top threads but only one bobbin thread, so the back of the work looks different.

◀ Add a row or two of decorative top stitching to plain shirts or blouses to give them a new lease on life. Choose contrasting threads and use the edge of the garment as a guide. Remember to sew a test piece first.

DECORATIVE FINISHES

Changing threads or adding cords and ribbons is another quick-and-easy way to achieve decorative top-stitched finishes.

▶ Try a few of the stitches on your machine. Work 1–2 rows, leaving minimal space (¼ in./ 6 mm) between the rows.

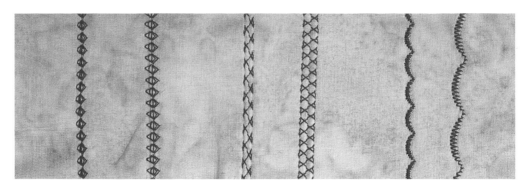

◀ Use a thicker, decorative thread, hand wound on the bobbin, and work with the underside of the item facing up. When turned over, the decorative thread will be on the right side.

GIMPING (COUCHING)

Gimping is a decorative finish that encases cords or ribbons.

◀ Place a thin cord or ribbon along the stitching line and machine stitch zigzag stitching over it, encasing the trim. Use the technique on hems, cuffs, or pocket edges to produce a designer finish.

▶ Once proficient at gimping, try creating patterns with cord and contrasting thread. Add the finish to an existing shirt collar or use it to decorate a plain cushion cover.

Pillow Power

Give your couch a new lease on life with a set of stunning throw pillows. These "envelope" covers are quick to make and need no zipper. Embellish them with decorative machine stitches for a touch of pizzazz!

STEP 1
▼ Cut the fabric into panels: one 16 in. (41 cm) square for the front and two 16 x 12 in. (41 x 30 cm) for the backs.

STEP 2
◄ Cut the interfacing 15 in. (38 cm) square, and center it on the wrong side of the front panel. Note that this is slightly smaller than the fabric panel, so it will not be in the seam allowances. Stitch close to the edge of the interfacing all around.

STEP 3 ◄ Using the dressmaker's carbon paper and tracing wheel, mark stitching lines on the right side of the interfaced panel. Here, I used simple squares. To center the design, find the fabric center by folding it in half and in half again, and crease.

TIP: *Press the decorated panel from the wrong side, using a press cloth to protect the work.*

STEP 4 ► Thread the sewing machine with contrasting machine embroidery thread and, starting at the inner edge of the pattern, sew the first row of top stitches. Continue working each line of stitches, changing colors as you proceed to create the design. Press.

STEP 5 ▼ ► Working with a back panel, turn one long edge under to the wrong side 1 in. (25 mm). Then turn the raw edge under again ¼ in. (6 mm). Press and machine stitch in place. Repeat for the other back panel. Press again.

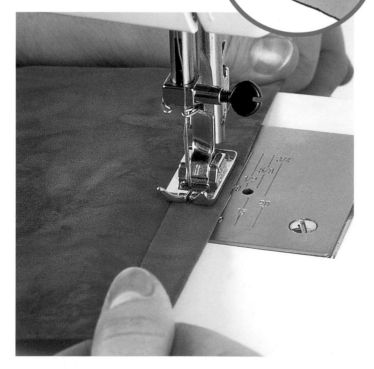

STEP 6 ▼ Place the front panel, right side up, on a clean work surface. Add one back panel, right side down, over the front, matching raw edges at top and sides. Place the other back panel, again right side down, matching raw edges at bottom and sides. (The back panels will overlap in the middle by approximately 4 in./10 cm.)

STEP 7 ▶ Pin all the layers together around the edges, placing pins at right angles so they are easy to remove as you stitch.

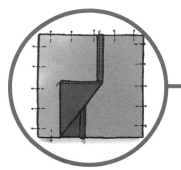

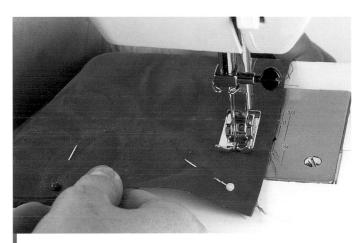

TIP: *When sewing single stitches, use the hand wheel on the side of the machine for greater control.*

STEP 8 ◀ Taking a ⅝-in. (15-mm) seam allowance and starting in the center of a side edge, machine stitch to the first corner, removing pins as you go. Backstitch/reverse stitch at the beginning to secure the thread. At the corner, stop with the needle in the work, raise the presser foot, pivot the work so the stitch will be on an angle, lower the presser foot, and make one stitch. Again, stop with the needle down, lift the presser foot, pivot the work to start the next side, lower the foot. Stitch to the next corner and repeat. Continue until you return to your start point. Backstitch/reverse stitch to secure stitches at the end.

STEP 9 ▶ Layer seam allowances by cutting the top edge to a scant ¼ in. (6 mm). Cut corners at an angle, close to the stitching. To finish raw side edges, zigzag or overcast stitch each edge.

OPTIONAL ▼

Add three snaps to the back panels, if desired. Space them equally across the width, and hand stitch the pointed half to the under panel and its partner to the upper panel.

STEP 10 ▲ Turn the cover to the right side, pushing out corners carefully with a point turner. Roll sides between finger and thumb to position seams on the edge. Press, using a press cloth to protect the decorative stitching.

TIP: *If the fabric frays easily, add a spot of fabric glue to the corners before turning through to the right side.*

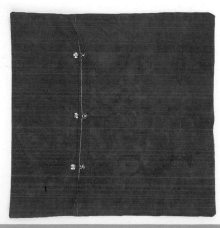

TRIMMINGS

Ribbons, braids, fringes, and laces can cover seams, trim pockets, and edge hems—and be a creative design detail at the same time.

Trimming methods depend on the kind of trim and its width. Trims can be positioned on an edge or a little way in, according to your preference. If wider than 3/8 in. (1 cm), the trim should be sewn along both its long edges—stitching both times in the same direction to prevent puckering. Narrow trims can be zigzag stitched down the center.

If your pattern does not give guidance, determine the amount of trim needed by measuring the areas to be trimmed and adding 1/2 yd. (46 cm) for joining ends, going around corners and curves, and so on. For very curved areas, choose a flexible trim, such as rickrack, bias tape, or knitted bands. Be sure to select a trim that needs the same type of laundering as the main fabric. For piping, see pages 92–95.

STEPS TO SEW

1 Position the trim, measuring from the outer edge at regular intervals to be sure of accuracy. Pin the trim in place so that the ends overlap slightly.

2 ▶ Gently pull back the top layer and start stitching from the pinned end. Machine stitch along the edge of the trim all the way around. Keep the trim relaxed to prevent puckering when it is stitched into place.

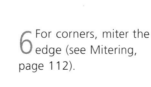

3 As you reach the overlap end, tuck the raw edge under and stitch it in place.

4 ▶ Machine stitch again, in the same direction, working on the other edge of the trim.

5 For curves, stop with the needle in, pivot slightly, and continue. Repeat as you work around the angle.

6 For corners, miter the edge (see Mitering, page 112).

7 Zigzag stitch narrow trims, working down the center of the trim.

8 Press in place using a press cloth.

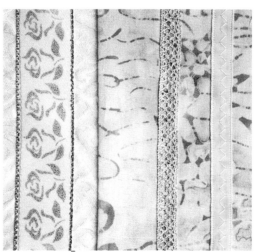

TIP: *If possible, add trims before the garment or project is sewn, so that the raw ends can be stitched in the seams.*

DECORATIVE EDGES

Use fringes, rickrack braid, or scalloped trims along the edges of hems or cuffs. Turn up the hem the desired amount, turning raw edges under to encase. Blind hem stitch or machine stitch and press. Add edging, either to the inside—so that fringing or a scalloped edge falls below the hemline—or to the outside edge if the tape is attractive. Pin the trim all around and machine stitch it in position, overlapping the edges as described above.

TIP. *If there are beads or sequins on the raw edge, cut or crush them to reduce the bulk in the turned-under raw edge.*

BEADED TRIMS

Some trims with beads or sequins are best sewn by hand unless you have the correct beading presser foot for your machine. Start at one side seam and tuck the raw edges of the trim under. Using small stitches, hand stitch between the beads or sequins—along the center of a trim that is under $^3/_8$ in. (3 mm) wide, and down both long edges of wider trims.

ADDING BEADS

◀ Make a plain trim more exotic by adding beads. Machine stitch the trim in place, as described above, and then hand stitch the beads at intervals, working the thread between the trim and the fabric between bead placement so that a long line of thread does not appear on the back of the work. Use a beading needle, which is often curved and has a very small eye.

Glamorize a plain evening top by adding a cluster of hand-stitched beads to collar points or the neckline.

INSERTIONS

See-through trims with double-edged detail, such as lace or eyelet, can be inserted into a garment and the fabric behind cut away. This looks effective and is not difficult to achieve.

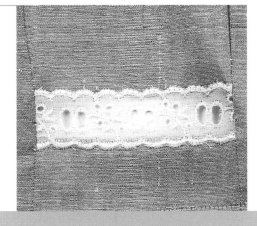

TIP: *Insert this trim before side seams are sewn, so that the ends can be included within the side seam allowance.*

1 Pin the trim in place and top stitch along both long edges. For scalloped edges, stitch just inside the curves so that the decorative edges remain free.

2 Turn to the wrong side and carefully cut away the fabric between the two rows of stitching. Press the seam allowance away from the trim, toward the fabric.

3 Return to the right side and edge stitch (top stitch close to the edge) through all layers.

4 ▶ Return to the wrong side and, using sharp embroidery scissors, trim seam allowances close to the stitching.

USING ELASTIC

There are many kinds of elastic, in many widths. Elastic is used in gathered waistbands, around the neckline of gypsy-style tops, in trousers, hats, and lingerie, and in the tops of bags. There are three main ways to use it: in a tunnel (known as a casing); by direct application, where the casing is created at the same time as the elastic is applied; or by machine stitching to the inside edges. For outer garments the elastic is usually inserted into casings, whereas for underwear, it can be added to edges.

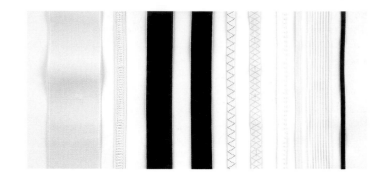

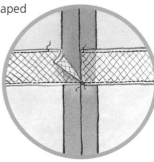

FORMING ELASTIC CASING

Casings are used at waistbands, pants leg edges, and sleeves. Printed patterns include an extended garment edge to use as the casing. If making your own pattern, add approximately 2 in. (5 cm) to the top edge for the casing.

1 Press the casing allowance to the wrong side, 2 in. (5 cm) from the top, tucking the raw edge under ¼ in. (6 mm).

2 ▶ Edge stitch close to both folded edges, leaving a 1½-in. (4-cm) gap in the lower edge to insert the elastic.

3 Determine the elastic length required: the body measurement less 1 in. (25 mm).

TIP: To prevent the elastic from twisting within the casing, machine stitch through all layers at the side seams.

4 ▶ Feed the elastic through the casing, using a safety pin or notions created for this purpose. Anchor the loose end outside the casing to make sure it doesn't disappear inside.

5 ▶ Safety pin both ends together—on the outside of the casing—and try the garment on for fit. Adjust as necessary before machine stitching both elastic edges together firmly.

6 Ease the stitched elastic ends into the casing and slip stitch the gap closed.

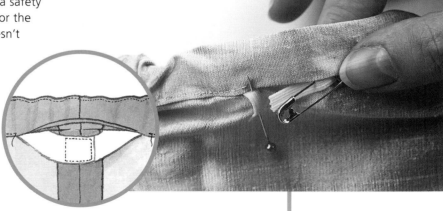

APPLIED CASING

▶ It is sometimes preferable to add a casing to minimize bulk on shaped edges or at the waistline of dresses. Use tricot seam binding, which eliminates the need to finish edges. Position binding where gathering is required (close to the top edge or at the waist mark). Stitch along both long edges. Insert elastic where the two ends meet, calculating the length of elastic required as described above.

TIP: To reduce bulk in the casing, overlock the raw edge of the fabric instead of turning under ¼ in. (6 mm). If using knit or tightly woven fabrics, finishing is unnecessary.

TIP: To prevent elastic from getting stuck in seam allowances during insertion, use fusible bonding to hold seam allowances down within the casing area.

DIRECT APPLICATION OF ELASTIC

This method stitches the elastic to the fabric while forming a casing at the same time, and prevents the elastic from curling or twisting. It is frequently used on the edge of a knitted garment, lingerie, or sportswear. It also uses the "quartering" method of application.

1 Cut the elastic to the required length (body measurement less 3 in. (8 cm). Overlap the ends and stitch them together, forming a continuous loop.

2 Trim the seam allowance to the same width as the elastic.

3 Divide the elastic into quarters. Do the same to the garment edge, dividing it into quarters.

4 ▶ Pin the elastic to the wrong side of the garment, matching any markings and keeping the edge of the elastic even with the raw edge of the garment.

TIP: *Divide the elastic and garment edge into eighths instead of quarters when first practicing the technique or when working on a long edge.*

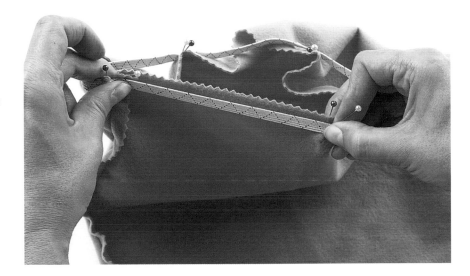

5 ◀ Stretching the elastic to match the quarters as you sew, zigzag stitch (or overcast) to the edge of the garment.

6 ▶ Fold the elastic to the inside of the garment and stitch through all layers, close to the raw edge, using a zigzag stitch, stretch stitch, or overcast stitch, and again stretching the elastic to match the quarters.

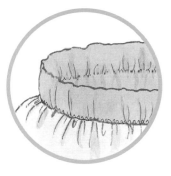

TIP: *You can apply exposed elastic using a serger (overlocker), which finishes the garment edge at the same time as stitching the elastic in place. Pin the straight edge of the elastic along the garment fold line at the quarter marks, and with elastic side up, position the straight elastic edge next to the blade. Stitch carefully, stretching the elastic as you go.*

EXPOSED APPLICATION OF ELASTIC

This application is most often used for lingerie. It is fast to apply and comfortable to wear. Because the elastic is exposed, use a soft, stretchy elastic with one picot or decorative edge—often referred to as lingerie elastic.

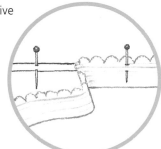

1 Finish the garment edge with an overcast or zigzag stitch, or by turning the raw edge to the inside and pressing.

2 Divide and mark the elastic into quarters or eighths. Repeat on the finished garment edge, as before.

3 ◀ Position the elastic with the straight edge along the finished garment edge. The elastic can be placed either on the right side of the garment or on the inside.

4 As before, stretch the elastic to match the quarters as you sew, using a zigzag or overcast stitch.

BALLERINA SKIRT

Little girls love to dress up as ballerinas, brides, or fairies. Make a pretty tulle (net) skirt and let their imagination take over! You can add ribbons and trims for an attractive finish.

YOU WILL NEED
For a child aged 5–6
- 1½ yd. (136 cm) fine double-width tulle (approximately 120 in./3m wide)*
- 1½ yd. of 54-in.-wide tulle (136 cm of 137-cm width) in a darker shade
- 3 yd. (276 cm) ribbons and trims
- ¾ yd. of ½-in.-wide elastic (69 cm of 13-mm width)
- 1¼ yd. of 2-in.-wide white ribbon (115 cm of 5-cm width)
- Sewing threads to match

EQUIPMENT
- Scissors
- Long, glass-head pins or paper clips**
- Sewing machine
- Large safety pin

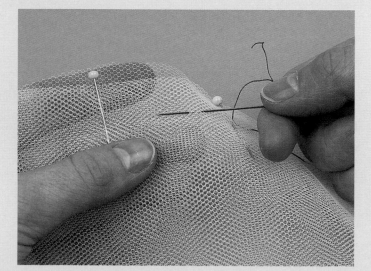

* Or 3 yd. of 52–54-in.-wide tulle (276 cm of 132–137 cm width)
** Colorful plastic paper clips are a good alternative to use on fabrics that are difficult to pin together.

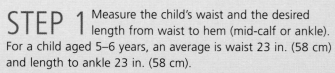

STEP 1 Measure the child's waist and the desired length from waist to hem (mid-calf or ankle). For a child aged 5–6 years, an average is waist 23 in. (58 cm) and length to ankle 23 in. (58 cm).

STEP 2 Cut the fine tulle into four pieces, each 54 in. (137 cm) wide and about 23 in. (58 cm) long— or to the length required. This can be done by folding the tulle in quarters, pinning the sides through all layers to hold them in place, and cutting as one.

STEP 3 ◄ Because tulle is springy, it will be easier to handle if it is basted together at the side edges before machine stitching. Use long hand basting stitches in a contrasting color thread that will be easy to remove later.

STEP 4 ▶ Fold the basted four-layered panel in half widthwise to form a tube, and pin at the basted edge through all layers, placing pins at right angles. Keep pins close to hold the layers in place.

STEP 5 Machine stitch the seam through all the layers, allowing a ⁵⁄₈-in. (15-mm) seam allowance. Trim seam allowances to ¼ in. (6 mm).

STEP 6 Fold the darker tulle in half to create two equal panels of 25 x 54 in. (64 x 137 cm), and again pin the layers together to hold them in place. Note that these panels are slightly longer than the fine tulle.

STEP 7 Stitch these two panels together at the side seams to form a tube, again taking a ⁵⁄₈-in. (15-mm) seam allowance and trimming it to ¼ in. (6 mm) when stitched.

STEP 8 Gather stitch around the top edge of the fine tulle by pulling up bobbin thread. Gather loosely to approximately 45 in. (114 cm). Repeat for the darker tulle.

STEP 9 ◀ Keeping the tube of darker tulle wrong side out, slip the fine tulle tube over it, with the wrong side in (so that the seam allowances are inside).

STEP 10 ▲ Pin the top edge of all layers together, adjusting gathers so they match in size, then machine baste to secure.

STEP 11 Sew the short ends of the 2-in. (5-cm) wide ribbon together and finish the raw edge.

STEP 12 ▶ Working from the wrong side of the garment, pin the right side of the ribbon top edge to the top of skirt, over the line of stitching. Machine stitch in place, close to the edge of the ribbon.

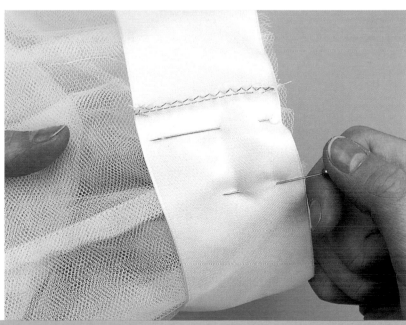

TIP: *To reduce bulk, turn the tubes so that their seams are on opposite sides, not together.*

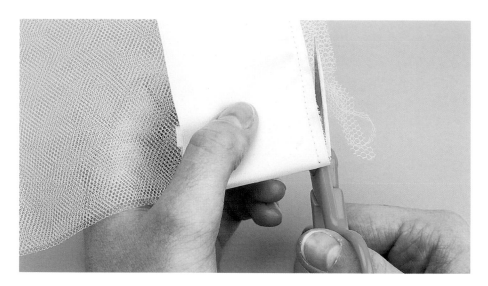

STEP 13 ◀ Trim the tulle to just above the ribbon edge.

STEP 14 ▼ Fold the ribbon in half to encase raw edges and form the casing for the elastic. Press with a damp cloth and pin in place.

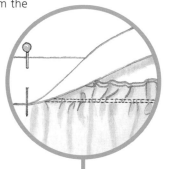

STEP 15 ▼ Working from the right side, machine stitch the ribbon to the skirt, through all thicknesses, close to the ribbon edge. Leave a gap of about 1 in. (25 mm) to feed the elastic through. Remember to backstitch/reverse stitch at the start and finish of the row of stitching.

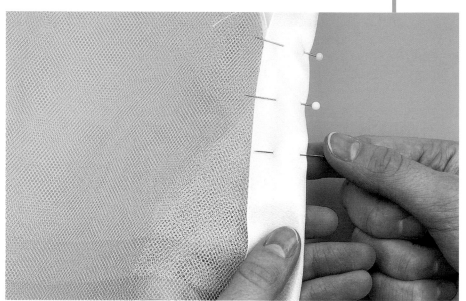

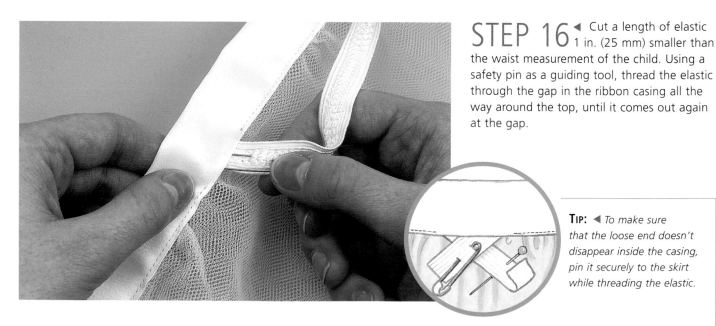

STEP 16 ◀ Cut a length of elastic 1 in. (25 mm) smaller than the waist measurement of the child. Using a safety pin as a guiding tool, thread the elastic through the gap in the ribbon casing all the way around the top, until it comes out again at the gap.

TIP: ◀ *To make sure that the loose end doesn't disappear inside the casing, pin it securely to the skirt while threading the elastic.*

STEP 17 ◄ Overlap the elastic ends and hand or machine stitch them together securely around all edges.

STEP 18 ► Pull on the gathered skirt top to hide the elastic ends inside. Hand slip stitch the gap closed. Adjust the gathers so that they fall evenly.

TIP: *To prevent the elastic from twisting in the casing, machine stitch through all thicknesses at the sides.*

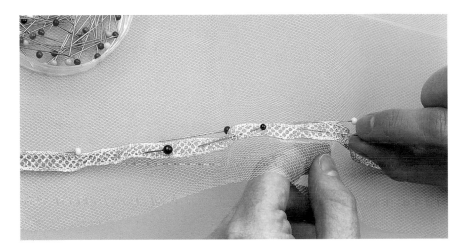

STEP 19 Check the length of the skirt against the little girl or her measurements. A pretty length is mid-calf or above the ankle. If necessary, trim the hem edge to the desired length.

STEP 20 ▼ Measure 1 in. (25 mm) and 2 in. (5 cm) from the hem edge on the top layer of tulle. Mark at intervals around the skirt, using pins.

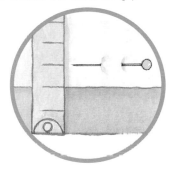

STEP 21 ▲ Pin one or two decorative ribbons and braids to the top layer of tulle at the marked points. Machine stitch in place. For narrow ribbons, one line of stitching down the middle is enough; for wider ribbons (over ½ in./13 mm), stitch along both edges. Overlap the ends slightly and, if they are liable to fray, tuck the raw end of the top length under and hand slip stitch in place.

TIP: *When stitching both edges of a trim, stitch both sides in the same direction to avoid puckering.*

DOUBLE THE FUN

Transform the ballerina skirt into a dress fit for a princess. Turn the skirt through so the darker tulle is on top. Note that this layer is slightly longer than the fine tulle. Measure and mark about 4 in. (10 cm) above the hemline. Pin trim in place and machine stitch to the upper layer.

TIP: ► *For an ethereal look, shape the hemline into feathery strips by cutting around a paper template.*

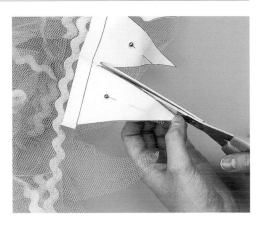

BIAS BINDING

Bias binding is used to finish raw edges by encasing them and to provide a decorative trim.

It can be applied at neck edges, armholes, and even hemlines. Bindings are often used in place of facings, especially on sheer, lightweight fabrics where facings can show through. They offer an easy way to finish reversible garments, such as jackets, vests, or capes, or to decorate placemats, napkins, tablecloths, and curtain edges.

The binding is referred to as "bias" because the fabric strips used to make it are cut on the bias—the stretchiest part of the fabric. This allows the binding to curve with the edge to be bound. Bias bindings can be purchased in a variety of widths and different fabric finishes, but it is easy to make your own, using various sizes of bias tapemaker. If a pattern calls for bias binding, check the notions to determine the recommended binding width. Most patterns are designed for a finished width of $1/4$–$1/2$ in. (6–13 mm).

The bias binding folds from one side to the other, encasing the trimmed raw edges, so the width used will depend on the fabric thickness to be encased. Generally, heavier fabrics need wider bias binding and fine cottons can be finished adequately with narrow tape.

PURCHASED BIAS TAPE

Bias tape can be purchased as regular double-fold bias tape or foldover braid. Either can be used to encase raw edges, and the choice will depend on the finished project. For a child's garment, contrasting colorful binding looks good, whereas for an edge-to-edge jacket, decorative foldover braid would be more suitable.

TIP: *Check that the binding requires the same laundry care as the main fabric.*

MAKING BIAS TAPE

Like bought tape, the fabric used for bias binding is best cut on the bias to provide flexibility.

1 To find the bias, cut a rectangle of fabric so that each side of the rectangle follows a thread of the fabric. The longer side of the rectangle can follow either the lengthwise or crosswise grain (see Cutting out, page 17).

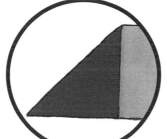

2◄ Working on the wrong side of the fabric, fold one corner of the rectangle so that the crosswise and lengthwise edges meet, and press. Open out. The crease is the true bias.

3 Cut a template from cardboard to the required width of your bias strips. Each strip should be four times the width of the finished binding. For example, for a ¼-in. (6-mm) finished binding width, cut strips 1 in. (25 mm) wide.

4◄ Starting at the crease and using the template as a guide, draw parallel lines across the width of the fabric.

5◄ Cut off the triangles at either end of the rectangle.

6 With right sides together, fold the fabric in half lengthwise, matching the pencil lines so that one width of binding extends beyond the edges on either side.

7▶ Stitch a ¼-in. (6-mm) seam to form a tube and press open the seam allowances.

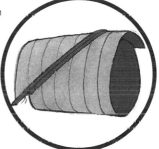

8 Starting at one end, cut along the marked line, working around the tube until it is one long strip of bias fabric.

9▶ To join strips of bias fabric to achieve the total length you need, place the ends of two strips with right sides together so that they form a 90° angle. (If you sew the strips with straight edges together they will not be flexible and bias at the join.) Sew the strips together, press the seam open, and trim away the points.

10▶ Use a bias tapemaker to fold the strips into binding. As you pull the strips through, they automatically fold. Work on an ironing board and steam press folds in place as you pull the fabric through.

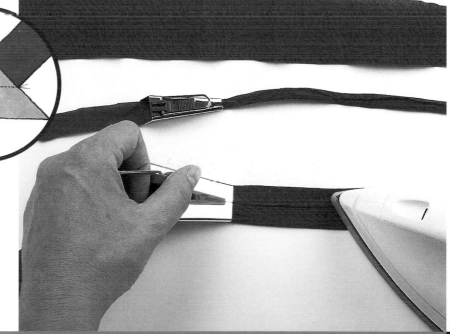

STEPS TO SEW

The usual way to apply binding is to pin and then stitch the opened binding to the stitching line on the right side of the garment. Fold the binding to the wrong side and then stitch in the ditch (the seam between garment and binding), catching the underside of the binding in place or slip stitching the underside by hand. For beginners, however, it is easier to use the following method:

1 Trim the garment seam allowance to a scant ¼ in. (6 mm).

2 ▶ Pin the opened bias tape to the wrong side of the garment, so that the opened fold line of the tape is on the seam line of the garment. Pin baste by inserting pins every 1–1½ in. (2.5–4 cm), or hand baste in position.

3 Carefully machine stitch along the basted line.

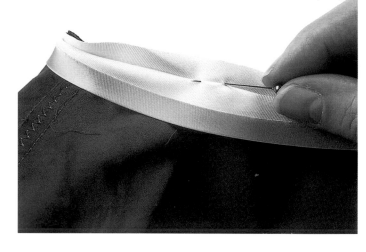

4 ◀ Turn the bias binding to the right side of the garment; press, then pin in place.

5 ▶ Top stitch close to the inner edge and press again.

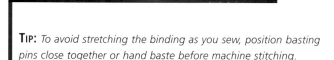

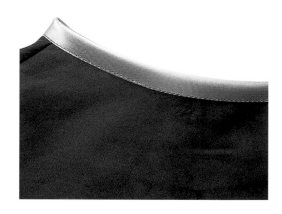

TIP: *To avoid stretching the binding as you sew, position basting pins close together or hand baste before machine stitching.*

JOINING ENDS

1 Press under one short end of the binding.

2 Start the binding at an inconspicuous area, such as a side seam or underarm. Pin and then stitch the pressed end in place, working all around the seam to be bound.

3 ▶ Lap the unpressed end over the pressed end. (Once the binding is folded over, the pressed edge will be uppermost.)

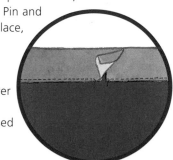

FOLDED BRAID

Folded braid binding is usually folded only once and does not have raw edges, so it is even easier to apply. Usually one edge of the braid is slightly wider than the other.

1 Sandwich the raw edges of the fabric to be bound with the folded braid, placing the wider edge on the bottom.

2 Working on the right side, edge stitch the braid in place.

3 To overlap binding neatly, tuck the raw edge of the end of the binding under and lap it over the unpressed end.

WORKING AROUND AN OUTSIDE EDGE

1 Mark the point where the seam allowances cross at the corner of the fabric.

2 With bias tape pinned to the edge as described above, stitch to the marking at the corner. Backstitch two or three times.

3 ▶ Fold the unstitched end of the bias binding back on itself to create a diagonal crease at the corner (with spare tape folded away from the fabric).

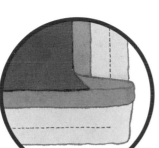

4 Fold the binding back again, so that the new fold is even with the raw edges of the binding and fabric.

5 Insert the needle exactly at the corner marking and continue stitching along the next edge. Repeat for each corner.

6 ▶ When done, fold the binding to the wrong side and slip stitch in place, stitching the corner fold also.

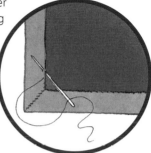

BINDING INSIDE CORNERS

1 ▶ Using small stitches, reinforce the corner at the seam line. Then clip the corner close to the stitches.

2 As before, stitch the binding to one edge until the corner is reached. Keeping the needle in the fabric, raise the presser foot and spread the fabric open at the clipped corner to line up with the binding edge.

3 ◀ Lower the presser foot and continue to stitch.

4 Press the seam allowances toward the binding. A diagonal of fabric will form at the corner.

5 Turn the binding to the inside, encasing raw edges and forming another diagonal fold. Finish the binding and slip stitch the corner folds.

OUTSIDE CORNERS OF FOLDED BRAID

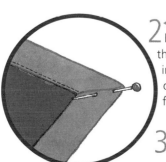

1 ▶ Stitch the braid to the end of the first row. Remove the fabric and cut the thread.

2 ◀ Turn the binding around the corner and pin it in position. Make a diagonal fold in the excess fabric on both front and back.

3 Start machine stitching again just below the diagonal, backstitching to secure.

INSIDE CORNERS OF FOLDED BRAID

1 As with bias binding, reinforce the corners and clip close to the stitching. Edge stitch the folded braid to the garment until the corner is reached. Stop with the needle down in the fabric.

2 Raise the presser foot and spread the fabric so it becomes a straight line. Slip the binding over the fabric, lower the presser foot, and continue stitching.

3 Press the binding, forming diagonals at the corner. Slip stitch in place.

Wonder Cape

A basic cape is the perfect costume topper—and a must for the superhero, devil, or vampire! This reversible cape is easy to make, and a great solution for last-minute costume occasions. The pattern size can be adjusted simply by cutting semicircles at the required length. Add bias binding to the side and collar edges for a quick, neat finish.

You will need
For a child aged 3–7
- 1 yd. of 36-in.-wide cotton or satin fabric (92 cm of 92-cm width), for outer layer
- 1 yd. of 36-in.-wide contrasting cotton or satin fabric (92 cm of 92-cm width), for inner layer
- 3½ yd. (322 cm) bias binding
- Vanishing marker pen or chalk pencil
- All-purpose sewing thread

Optional
- Snap fastener

Equipment
- Scissors and pins
- Long pin or knitting needle
- ¾ yd. (69 cm) string (for measuring)
- Sewing machine

STEP 1 If necessary, cut the fabric for the outer layer to a 36-in. (92-cm) square. Fold the square in half and pin through to hold the two halves together at the top, sides, and lightly in the center.

STEP 2 ◀ Tie one end of the string to a long safety pin (or use a knitting needle or pencil). Tie the vanishing marker pen (or chalk pencil) to the other end of the string, at the length required (neck to hem edge—length determined by the child's height and the length desired). Stick the pin into the folded corner of the fabric.

STEP 3 Check that the length of the string, when held taut, is the length required. If necessary, wrap any excess around the pin.

STEP 4 ▶ Holding the pin in position, draw from the folded side to the other edge, forming an arc.

STEP 5 ▼ Cut through both thicknesses along the arc line.

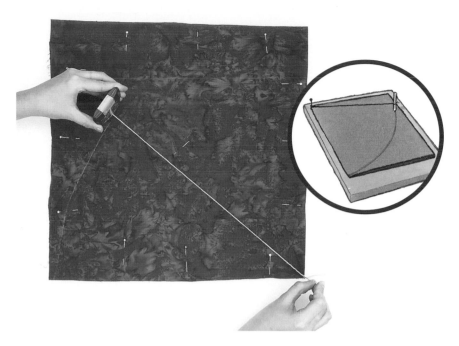

STEP 6 ▶ To make the curved neck edge, place a small plate (7 in./18 cm in diameter) at the top folded corner, so that approximately one-third is on the fabric. Again, using the vanishing marker pen (or chalk pencil), draw around the plate.

STEP 7 ◀ Cut through all thicknesses to remove excess fabric from the neck edge. Unpin and open out. Repeat steps 1–7 for the fabric for the inner layer.

STEP 8 ▼ Stay stitch the curved neck of each layer, stitching 1/4 in. (6 mm) from the raw edge, working slowly. Pivot work, as necessary, to prevent stretching as you stitch.

STEP 9 ◀ Pin the two fabric layers, right sides together, all around, matching raw edges. Starting at the bottom edge and taking a 1/4-in. (6-mm) seam allowance, machine stitch the layers together along the hem edge only. Clip the seam allowance all around. Remove pins and turn through to the right side. Roll the stitched edge between finger and thumb to get the seam to lie on edge. Press.

TIP: *To stitch a 1/4-in. (6-mm) seam allowance, put the needle in the center position and use the right edge of the presser foot as a guide along the raw edge. Alternatively, you can measure 1/4 in. (6 mm) from the needle position and mark the machine with a piece of masking tape to use as a guide.*

STEP 10 ▶ With wrong sides together, join the layers, pinning away from the edges. Starting at the top left edge, pin bias binding to the front edge of the fabric, matching raw edges. Continue pinning tape down to the bottom edge, tucking raw edges under. Machine stitch in place. Repeat for the right side.

STEP 11 ◀ Fold the bias binding to the other side of the cape, encasing raw edges. Pin in place and then machine stitch close to the tape edge.

STEP 12 ◀ Cut a length of bias binding 20 in. (50 cm) longer than the curved neck edge.

STEP 13 ◀ Starting with a 10-in. (25-cm) tail, pin bias binding to the wrong side of the left neck edge, matching raw edges as before. Continue around the neckline, pinning as you go. Machine stitch in place.

TIP: *Bias binding can be pinned and stitched in one step. Pin folded bias binding over the edge, encasing raw edges and checking that both sides of the binding are captured by the pins. Carefully stitch, close to the binding edge.*

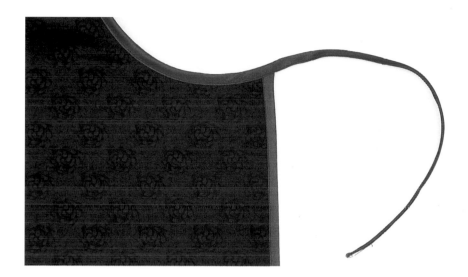

STEP 14 ◄ To finish the ends, fold the bias binding in half, right sides together, and stitch across the ends. Trim and turn through.

STEP 15 ► Fold the tape over to the right side of the cape and pin in place. Starting at the left tail end, stitch close to the edges through all thicknesses, continuing around the neck edge and down the right tail.

STEP 16 Remove all the pins.

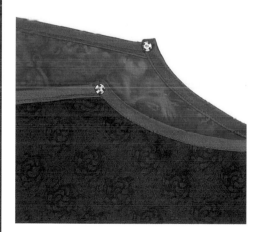

TIP: ▲ *For young children, replace the bias binding ties with a single snap fastener, hand stitched to the neck edge.*

TECHNIQUE TIP

I suggest attaching bias binding to the wrong side of the garment first, folding it over to the right side, and finishing by machine stitching from the right side, because this method is easiest for beginners. Once you are more confident, however, the favored technique is:

- Attach bias binding to the right side first.
- Machine stitch the open binding in place.
- Fold the binding over to the wrong side, encasing raw edges.
- Stitch in the ditch from the right side, catching the underside as you stitch.
- Alternatively, finish from the wrong side with a hand slip stitch.

Another method, once you are confident in controlling stitch direction, is to pin and stitch in one step. Pin folded bias binding over the raw edges, encasing them and pinning so that both sides are captured. Then machine stitch close to the binding edge, catching the underside at the same time.

BUTTONHOLES

Today's sewing machines make the process of creating buttonholes relatively simple. A stitched buttonhole consists of a bar tack—repeated stitching on the same spot at either end—and two close rows of tiny zigzag satin stitches. The order in which these are stitched depends upon the machine. The hole is then manually cut between the rows of tight satin stitches.

In one-step buttonholing you tell the machine the length of buttonhole you want, position the fabric under the foot, press "start," and away goes the machine, completing the bar tacks and rows automatically.

In a three-step buttonhole function you must change the dial or switch between steps: from bar tack to first satin stitch row, back to bar tack, and back to second row. It might also be necessary to turn the fabric around so that you stitch in the correct direction. Check your user manual to determine the method applicable to your machine.

▶ Buttonholes can be keyhole-shaped, straight-ended, rounded, or bound, but the basic buttonhole shown here is the easiest to make and the most widely used.

MEASURING SIZE
The length of the buttonhole depends on the shape of button. A domed button, for example, requires a larger buttonhole than a flat button, even if the diameter of both is identical.

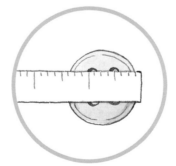

1 ◀ For flat buttons, measure the diameter of the button. Add to this ⅛ in. (3 mm), so that the button can slip in and out easily.

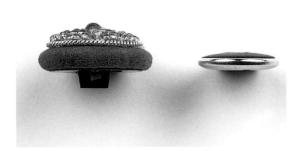

2 ▶ For domed or other shaped buttons, wrap a piece of ribbon around the widest part of the button and pin the ends together. The length of the buttonhole should be one-half of this circumference plus ⅛ in. (3 mm). Make a test buttonhole and try the button— if it is very thick, you may have to increase the length slightly.

Marking buttonhole placement

A row of buttonholes must be equally sized and perfectly in line. If using a bought pattern, transfer the placement lines from the tissue paper to the right side of the fabric. If making your own pattern, or adding buttons to cushions or bags, follow these guidelines:

Tip: *To gauge the correct distance between buttons, pin the layers together at regular intervals before marking the final positions of the buttonholes.*

1 Mark placement lines at least ³/₄ in. (2 cm) from the edge of the fabric.

2 ▶ For a row of vertical buttonholes, baste a straight line ³/₄ in. (2 cm) from the fabric edge, and then baste the buttonhole position/length at regular intervals at right angles to the vertical line, so that each one is the same size.

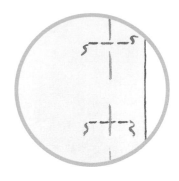

3 ◀ For a row of horizontal buttonholes, baste two rows of straight stitching, parallel to each other, with the distance between them equal to the buttonhole length. Then baste the buttonhole positions at equal distances between the straight rows.

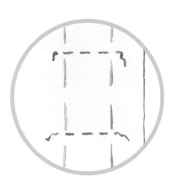

4 For clothes, an average gap between buttonholes is 2¹/₂–3 in. (6–8 cm). On soft furnishings, a distance of 4–5 in. (10–13 cm) is adequate.

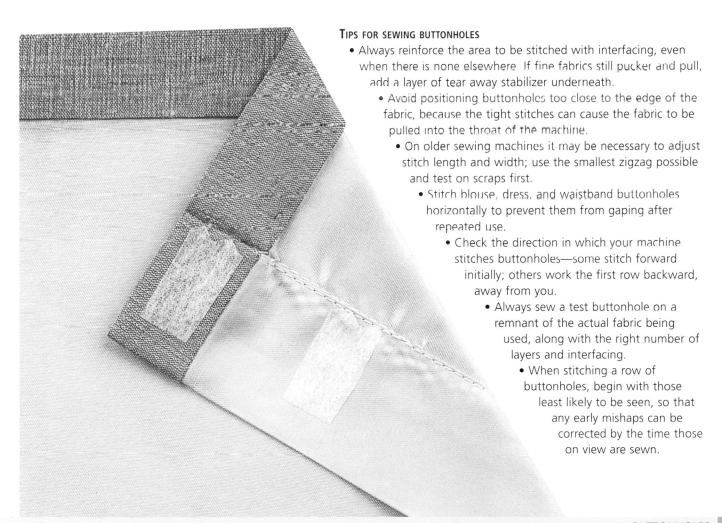

Tips for sewing buttonholes

• Always reinforce the area to be stitched with interfacing, even when there is none elsewhere. If fine fabrics still pucker and pull, add a layer of tear away stabilizer underneath.

• Avoid positioning buttonholes too close to the edge of the fabric, because the tight stitches can cause the fabric to be pulled into the throat of the machine.

• On older sewing machines it may be necessary to adjust stitch length and width; use the smallest zigzag possible and test on scraps first.

• Stitch blouse, dress, and waistband buttonholes horizontally to prevent them from gaping after repeated use.

• Check the direction in which your machine stitches buttonholes—some stitch forward initially; others work the first row backward, away from you.

• Always sew a test buttonhole on a remnant of the actual fabric being used, along with the right number of layers and interfacing.

• When stitching a row of buttonholes, begin with those least likely to be seen, so that any early mishaps can be corrected by the time those on view are sewn.

CUTTING OPEN A BUTTONHOLE

Once all the buttonholes are stitched, carefully slice them open between the rows of satin stitch. Place a pin at one end and, starting at the other end, use a buttonhole cutter, cutting through all layers. If whiskers of fabric appear, snip them very carefully and treat edges with a thin beading of fabric glue.

TIP: *If you do not have a buttonhole cutter, you can use a seam ripper or a pair of small sharp scissors, but start in the middle with the scissors and insert a pin at either end to prevent snipping too far.*

TIP: *If you accidentally cut into any stitches, apply a dot of seam sealant or fabric glue.*

TIP: *When using glue on delicate areas, apply with a fine paintbrush or pin to prevent seepage.*

POSITIONING BUTTONS

▶ Pin layers of fabric to be fastened as if the buttons were already applied, and then mark button placement as follows:

1 For a vertical buttonhole, insert a pin ⅛ in. (3 mm) from the top of the hole through to the under layer.

2 For a horizontal button, insert a pin ⅛ in. (3 mm) from the outer end.

SEWING ON BUTTONS

Sewing on buttons is a simple task, but there are ways to speed the process and hold the buttons more securely.

▶ Buttons come in two styles: with a shank and sew-through. The shank is designed to help buttons sit properly when passed through layers of fabric, so sew-through buttons need to have a shank added.

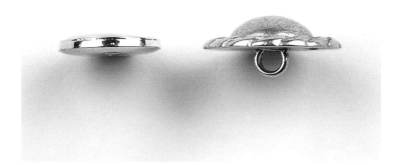

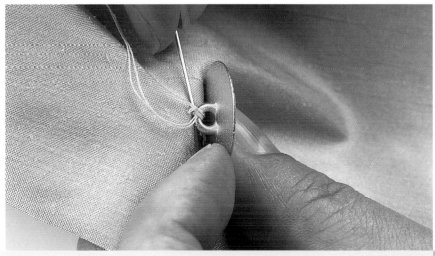

SEW-THROUGH

1 Thread a needle with a double strand of thread and make a few small backstitches at the pin position.

2 ◀ Hold a wooden matchstick or toothpick on top of the button and then bring the needle up through one buttonhole and down through another into the fabric, sewing over the matchstick. Repeat several times.

3 Remove the matchstick and, holding the button away from fabric, wind the thread around the excess thread below the button.

4 Stitch back into the fabric and backstitch to secure. Then "tunnel" the thread: Insert the needle between the fabric layers for about 1 in. (25 mm), bring the needle out, and pull taut. Snip the thread close to the fabric and let the ends disappear inside.

SHANK

1 Thread a needle with a double strand of thread and take a few small backstitches at the pin position.

2 ▶ Sew through the shank, catching the fabric on either side. Repeat several times. Backstitch 3–4 stitches and then "tunnel" the thread between fabric layers as above.

BAGS OF STYLE

Make an evening bag to match your outfit for a truly individual look. A bag can also be a fine gift, decorated with trims and embroidery to fit the occasion. This easy style can be made bigger or smaller to suit its purpose. There are many trims to choose from, including patterned braids, Lurex and satin bindings, metallic stars, feathers in jewel colors, silky cords, and ribbons. Add some simple machine embroidery to create a unique design.

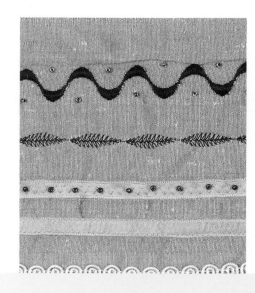

YOU WILL NEED
- 20 x 10 in. (50 x 25 cm) raw silk
- 20 x 10 in. (50 x 25 cm) lining fabric (polyester satin)
- 20 x 10 in. (50 x 25 cm) heavyweight sew-in interfacing (cut into two pieces, 10 in./ 25 cm square)
- 1 yd. (92 cm) bias binding
- 1³/₈ yd. (127 cm) silky cord
- 1 decorative button

Optional
- Decorative trims (10 in./25 cm lengths of each)
- Beads
- Seam sealant/fabric glue

EQUIPMENT
- Scissors and pins
- Seam ripper
- Sewing machine

STEP 1 Cut the main fabric into two 10 in. (25 cm) squares. Repeat for the lining and interfacing.

STEP 2 ◀ Pin and baste interfacing to the wrong side of both pieces of the main fabric.

STEP 3 ◀ Decorate the front panel with strips of braid, ribbons, or trims, sewn from edge to edge. Try out different combinations before sewing in place.

STEP 4 ▶ Add lines of embroidery in contrasting or gold thread (built-in stitches are available on most machines). Attach some small beads by hand.

STEP 5 ▶ Place one lining piece over the front panel, right sides together. Machine stitch along the top edge. Turn through to the right side, and press. Repeat with the other lining piece and the back panel.

STEP 6 ▶ Pin the front lined panel on top of the back lined panel, with linings together, at the sides and the bottom. Increase the stitch length on the sewing machine (approximately 1/8 in./3 mm) and machine stitch from the top right edge around to the top left edge, pivoting at corners.

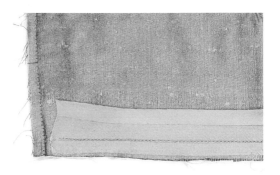

STEP 7 ◀ Bind the lower edge with bias binding by pinning and stitching the binding, the raw edge matching the bottom edge of the bag panels. Turn the tape to the right side and machine stitch close to the tape edge.

STEP 8 ▼ Bind the two side edges, as before, tucking under the binding by 1/2 in. (13 mm) at each corner.

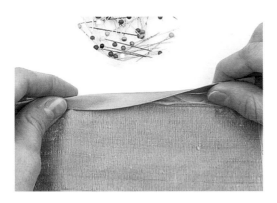

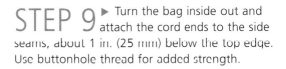

STEP 9 ▶ Turn the bag inside out and attach the cord ends to the side seams, about 1 in. (25 mm) below the top edge. Use buttonhole thread for added strength.

STEP 10 ▼ Mark the position for the buttonhole on the center front. The buttonhole is stitched vertically to prevent it pulling open when the bag is full. Machine stitch the buttonhole to match the size of the chosen button.

STEP 11 Mark the position of the button inside the back panel with a pin. Sew the button in place, taking care not to show any stitches on the outside.

TIP: To cover any stitches coming through, position an extra (flat) button at the same spot on the outside of the back panel.

TIP: Always test a sample buttonhole on the same combination of fabric/interfacing used for the project.

STEP 12 ▲ Hand stitch beaded trim to the top and bottom of the bag.

HEMMING

Clothes and soft furnishings can be hemmed by hand, by machine, and by fusing. The choice depends upon the fabric being stitched and the final look desired.

Hemming is usually the last stage in a project and should preferably be left until the garment or drapes have hung for at least 24 hours. This allows for the natural drop of the fabric; if it is uneven, the delayed hemming can straighten the edges. Hanging is especially important for knit garments or those with a bias cut.

HEM DEPTHS
The depth of the hem gives weight to the lower edge and enables the garment or curtain to hang properly.

- For straight dresses, skirts, and coats, an average hem depth is 2–3 in. (5–8 cm).

- For A-line or flared garments, an average hem allowance is 1¼–2 in. (3–5 cm).

- For pants, the average hem allowance is 1¼ in. (3 cm).

- For drapes, the average hem depth ranges from 2–4 in. (5–10 cm).

MEASURING HEM LENGTH
▶ Measure up from the floor to the hem level—not from the waist down, which may fail to account for figure shaping. Mark the hem with chalk, or with pins placed horizontally, along or around the hemline.

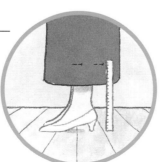

TIP: *If you plan to wear high heels with the finished garment, put those shoes on when measuring the hem, to be sure that the hem is even all around.*

NEEDLES AND THREADS
For hand hemming, use a small, thin needle that will not make holes in the fabric. Use all-purpose thread on cottons, polyesters, and wool blends, and silk thread on silks. Choose a color that is the same as or slightly darker than the fabric (thread looks lighter when sewn).

Cut thread length to a maximum 22 in. (56 cm). If the thread is inclined to knot, run it through tailor's wax, which will help it slip smoothly through the fabric. Use single strands on lightweight fabrics and double strands on heavyweight fabrics.

PREPARING HEM ALLOWANCE

▶ Turn the hem allowance up, matching the side seams. Insert pins at right angles close to the folded edge. Try on the garment again, to double-check accuracy. Measure and mark the hem allowance plus ¼ in. (6 mm) for finishing (see Hem depths, opposite). Trim off excess fabric.

EASING IN EXCESS

If the garment edge is slightly curved or A-line, the hem allowance will have extra fullness. This needs to be eased in to prevent ripples from forming.

1 After trimming the hem allowance, ease the stitch ¼ in. (6 mm) from the edge with a slightly loosened tension.

2◀ Place the garment on a flat surface and pull up the excess fabric, using the bobbin thread. Spread the fabric evenly and pin in place.

3 For full-skirted and circular hems, hand baste ¼ in. (6 mm) from the folded edge.

BIAS BINDING HEM

▶ Adding a bias binding or stretch lace tape to the hem edge compensates for a shortage of fabric. It also makes stitching a curved hem easier and looks professional. Satin bias tape is less bulky than cotton and makes a good choice for heavyweight fabrics. Stretch lace is especially suitable for lightweight fabrics.

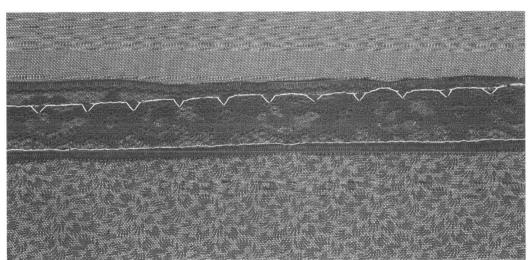

1 Measure hem length, as above.

2◀ Before turning up the hem allowance, machine stitch one long edge of the bias tape ¼ in. (6 mm) from the raw edge, working on the right side of the fabric. Press.

3▶ Turn up the hem allowance at the hem marking and blind stitch bias tape to the main fabric as before.

BLIND-STITCHED HEMS

▼ Blind stitching is the most widely used hemming technique. It can be done entirely by hand (see page 34) or by finishing the raw edge by machining first, as here. Blind stitching gives a slightly rounded hemline, but this can be pressed to a crisp edge. Pressing must be done carefully, however, to avoid the machine-stitched edge showing as a ridge on the right side.

TIP: *Every ten stitches or so, backstitch in the hem allowance to secure it, so that if the hem comes down, it will not do so completely.*

1 Measure the hem length up from the floor, as described above, marking all around.

2 If the amount of fabric hanging below the hem marking is greater than about 2 in. (5 cm) for garments or 4 in. (10 cm) for drapes (see Hem depths, page 74), cut off the excess.

3 Finish the raw edge using zigzag stitch, overcast, or overlock. Press the stitched edge to set the stitches.

4 Turn up the hem to the wrong side along the hem marking. Pin it in place.

5 Starting at a seam, fold back the machine-stitched edge and backstitch in the seam allowance to secure the stitches.

6 ◀ Take a stitch in the turned-back hem allowance and then a very small stitch, picking up only one or two threads in the body of the fabric. Repeat along the hem length, being careful not to pull the thread too tight.

7 When finished, allow the machine-stitched edge to roll back over the stitching.

8 Without pressing, steam the hem from the wrong side to set it in place.

TIP: ▶ *Many machines have a blind stitch presser foot and stitch to simplify the task (refer to your sewing machine manual for instructions). However, even a tiny stitch will show on the right side. Use matching thread to minimize showthrough.*

NARROW TOP-STITCHED HEMS

▶ Top-stitching is probably the quickest hemming method, because it is machine sewn and the raw edges do not need finishing (they are tucked inside). However, top-stitched hems should be used only on garments that have other top stitching detail.

For lightweight cottons and polyesters, and light woolens, the hem allowance should be double the hem depth, so that the raw edges are folded down to meet the first hem fold. For knits that do not unravel, the raw edge can be cut off ⅝ in. (15 mm) from the hem marking.

1 Measure the hem length as before, and fold up at the hem marking.

2 ▶ Tuck the raw edge under to meet at the fold.

3 Pin and press in place.

4 Machine stitch close to the edge of the hem allowance. If desired, machine stitch again, working in the same direction, close to the garment edge.

TIP: *It is preferable to work from the right side. However, if working from the wrong side in order to follow the hem allowance edge, make sure the bobbin thread is a perfect match for the fabric, since this will be the visible side.*

WIDE TOP-STITCHED HEMS

◀ These wide hems can be used on most fabrics and garment types, apart from those that would need a very curved hem. The usual hem allowance is 1½–2 in. (4–5 cm).

1 Measure, mark, and press the hem allowance up along the hemline.

2 On woven fabrics, tuck the raw edge under ½ in. (13 mm).

3 ◀ Working from the wrong side, machine stitch close to the edge of the hem allowance.

4 Stitch again, working in the same direction, ¼ in. (6 mm) from the first row of stitching.

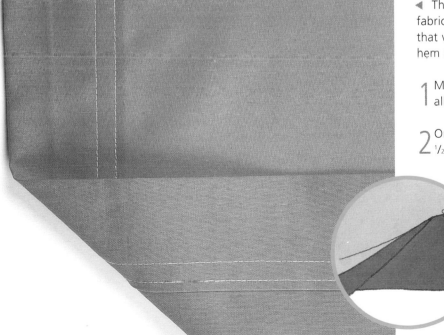

ROLLED HEMS

▶ A good choice for stretchy or sheer fabrics, rolled hems can be hand- or machine-stitched.

1 Measure the hem length ¹⁄₈ in. (3 mm) longer than the desired length.

2 Trim the hem allowance to ⁵⁄₈ in. (15 mm).

HAND-STITCHED

▶ Stretch the fabric slightly, so that the fabric curls inward, and then let it relax into a natural roll. Catch the stitch as before, picking up just one or two threads of the main fabric.

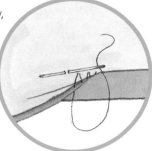

MACHINE-STITCHED

1 ▶ Fold up a narrow hem allowance and machine stitch ¹⁄₈ in. (3 mm) from the hemline. Trim close to the stitching.

2 Fold the hem allowance up along the stitched line, rolling the stitching slightly to the wrong side. Press.

3 ▶ Stitch again, working in the same direction, close to the inner fold.

SERGED EDGE

▽ This type of hem is quick to achieve and uses the thread as the edge. It is a good finish for lightweight to medium-weight woven fabrics. Do it with a serger, or recreate the look on a sewing machine. Always check the stitch size on a spare piece of fabric first.

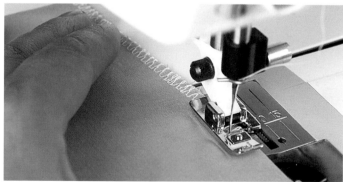

1 ▲ Use the buttonhole foot, with grooves on the bottom.

2 Set the stitch to a very small zigzag. Position the raw edge of the fabric under the foot, slightly to the right of center.

3 Sew with the left swing of the needle into the fabric and the right swing just outside the cut edge. As the needle moves from left to right, the thread will coax the fabric into a roll.

LETTUCE EDGE

◄ Lettuce edging is also best achieved with a serger. However, it can be done on a sewing machine when working with stretchy fabrics or lightweight fabrics cut on the bias. It is a delicate edging that looks great on ruffles and lingerie.

1 Set the machine to a zigzag stitch at ¹/₅₀ in. (0.5 mm) long and ⅛ in. (3 mm) wide. Position the fabric so that the left needle position stitches the fabric and the right is just off the cut edge.

2 Begin stitching, holding the fabric firmly in front of the machine so that it is stretched as it is sewn.

RUFFLED HEMS

▼ Ruffles are made from long lengths of fabric, gathered and then stitched to plain edges. Choose a quick method to hem the fabric to be ruffled, such as top stitching, machine rolling, or lettuce edging. Hem just one edge. The ruffle can then be gathered in the same way as other garment areas (see Gathering, page 40). To attach a ruffled trim to a hemline, follow these simple steps:

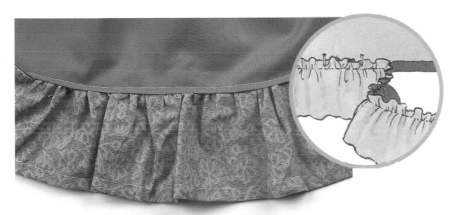

1 Measure the hem length as before, deducting the depth of the ruffle.

2 Turn up the hem on the hemline, measuring a ⅝-in. (15-mm) hem allowance. Trim the excess fabric. Press the allowance to the wrong side.

3◄ With right sides up, pin the ruffle to the garment edge, lapping the pressed edge of the garment over the ruffle and matching the raw edges underneath. Adjust the ruffle gathers to distribute fullness evenly.

4 Edge stitch close to the fold through all layers.

5 Finish the raw edge of the ruffle by overcasting, zigzagging, or pinking.

HEM WEIGHTS

Hem weights are used, literally, to add weight to the hem. They help drapes hang properly and can be used in garments such as coats and jackets to improve the finished look. Hem weights are usually added within the hem allowance before hemming.

The weights can be disks or tape. Disks are sewn just within the edges at the sides. The added weight at these specific points helps prevent curtains or coats from curling up at the edges. Hem weight tape is a series of little lead weights encased in netting. In wide top-stitched hems, the tape can be fed through the hem allowance after the hem is stitched. Alternatively, place the tape inside the hem allowance along the fold line as you stitch. Catch stitch the tape to the side seams to secure.

LINING HEMS

Linings can have a machine-stitched hem and are usually double hemmed. ▶ Lined garments, such as jackets, have a lining stitched to the main fabric and facings all the way around. ▼ Skirts, dresses, coats, and drapes have a lining that hangs separately. The lining hem should be shorter than the main fabric hem, so that it doesn't hang below. Position the lining hem to sit just over the top of the main fabric hem fold.

TIP: *Before making lined curtains or garments, prewash the fabric and lining to prevent uneven shrinkage at later laundering.*

HEM ALTERATIONS

Altering and repairing hems are probably the most frequent hand-sewing activities—and can transform the look of a garment.

TIP: *If the fabric unravels easily, finish the raw edge with an overcast, overlock, or zigzag stitch before hemming.*

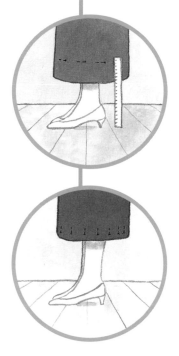

SHORTENING

You will shorten an item of your own clothing more accurately if someone else pins up the hem while you are wearing the garment. This will ensure that it is the correct length to suit your posture.

1 ◄ Check that the wearer's shoes are those usually worn with the garment. Then, starting at the back, measure from the floor up to the new length required, marking the position with a pin or chalk pencil. Repeat for the front and sides.

2 ◄ Turn excess fabric to the wrong side along the marked line and pin it in position to check the hem level.

3 ► Place the garment inside out on a flat surface and mark the new hem allowance. Measure 1½ in. (4 cm) up from the new fold line. Trim off any excess fabric.

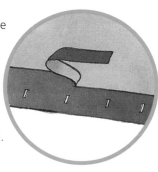

4 Turn the raw edge under ½ in. (13 mm) to encase it, and press in place. Blind stitch the hem edge to the garment, easing in any extra fullness as you stitch.

LENGTHENING

Lengthening the hemline of children's clothes can give a few extra months of wear.

1 Unpick the original hem stitch carefully, using a seam ripper, and unfold the hem allowance, leaving the raw edge tucked under, if applicable.

2 Press with a steam iron and damp cloth to remove the fold in the fabric.

3 Try on the garment and mark the new hemline, as above. Fold the hem to the wrong side and press. Blind hem stitch, as before, or top stitch, working from the right side.

TIP: *Hide any discoloration or marking on the original fold line with a decorative trim or fringe. Machine stitch in place along both edges of the trim, stitching each edge in the same direction.*

STRAIGHTENING

Bias-cut and loose-knit garments tend to sag unevenly after a while. To adjust the hem, first mark the length of the shortest part, again working from floor to hem.

1 ◄ Mark the same measurement from the floor to the new hemline at the sides, back, and front of the garment. Fold up the excess to the wrong side and pin in place all around to check levels.

2 ► Working on a flat surface, mark the new hem allowance evenly all around and then trim off the uneven, excess fabric.

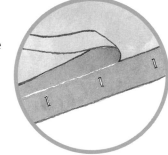

3 Finish the raw edge and blind stitch, as before.

QUICK FIX

◄ Use a fusible bonding to stick the hem in position. This is a double-sided adhesive web that is sandwiched between the hem allowance and the main fabric and fused in place using a steam iron and press cloth.

TIP: *Allow the fabric to cool completely before handling to help the adhesive stick.*

SUMMER SHORTS

Simple shorts are perfect for fun days in the sun. This design is easy to make and can be enlarged or reduced for different ages and sizes.

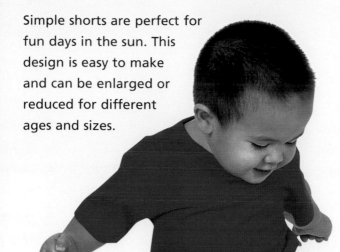

It is important when using any pattern to fold the fabric as recommended and to place the pattern pieces so that the grain line markings match the grain of the fabric. One of the biggest errors is to work with the fabric off grain, causing it to twist at the seams, bag, or stretch unevenly (see Cutting out, page 17).

Some patterns include seam allowances, for others you must add them. They are usually between ¼ in. (6 mm) and ⅝ in. (15 mm), unless otherwise stated. This pattern has seam allowances of ¼ in. (6 mm) included in the pattern sizing.

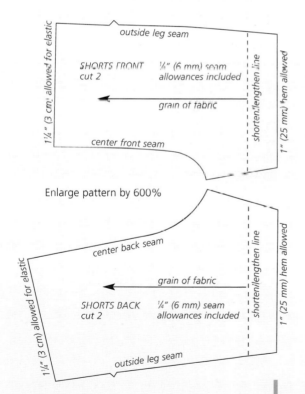

Enlarge pattern by 600%

INCREASING PATTERN SIZE

The pattern used here is for children aged 2–3 years, height 35–38 in. (89–97 cm), waist 20–20½ in. (51–52 cm). For larger sizes, increase the pattern all around by ⅜ in. (1 cm) for each successive age, as follows:

Age	Add	Height	Waist
4–5	⅜ in. (1 cm) all around	41–44 in. (104–112 cm)	21–21½ in. (53–55 cm)
6	⅜ in. (1 cm) all around	47 in. (119 cm)	22 in. (56 cm)
7–8	¾ in. (2 cm) all around	50–52 in. (127–132 cm)	23–23½ in. (58–60 cm)
10	1⅛ in. (3 cm) all around	56 in. (142 cm)	24½ in. (62 cm)
12	1½ in. (4 cm) all around	58½ in. (149 cm)	25½ in. (65 cm)

TIP: *Keep paper pattern pieces folded with fabric pieces and within easy reach for reference, if needed, as you sew.*

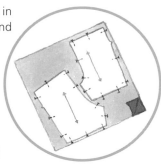

STEP 1 ▶ Fold the fabric in half, right sides and selvages together, and pin the pattern pieces as shown in the diagram (right).

STEP 2 Cut out through both thicknesses of fabric, cutting around the notches. Remove the pattern and mark the right side of the fabric.

STEP 3 ◀ Pin one front to one back piece at the inner leg seams, right sides together. Stitch the seam, slightly stretching the back to fit. Repeat for the other leg.

STEP 4 ▶ With the right sides of the fabric together, pin the center seam, matching the inner leg seams. Stitch. Reinforce the stitching by sewing again over the first row of stitching.

STEP 5 ▶ Trim the curved area to a scant ⅛ in. (3 mm) and press the remainder of the seam allowance open.

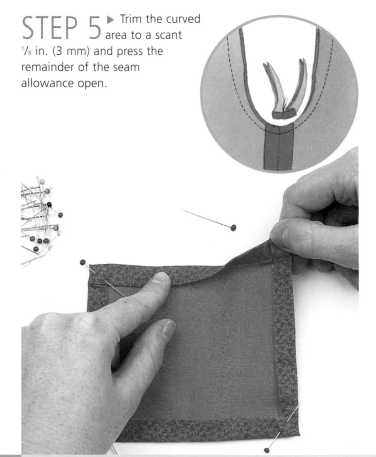

STEP 6 ▶ Stitch the front piece to the back piece at the side seam, matching notches. Repeat for the other leg.

POCKET

STEP 7 ◀▶ Cut a fabric square of 5 in. (13 cm). Turn raw edges to the wrong side ¼ in. (6 mm) all around, first folding corners in at an angle. Press. Turn the top edge under again ¼ in. (6 mm) to encase raw edges and top stitch in place.

STEP 8 ▼
Place the pocket on the back, in the position marked. Using your machine's free-arm (taking the accessory box off to leave a thinner base), machine stitch the pocket in place around three sides, backstitching at corners to reinforce the stitching.

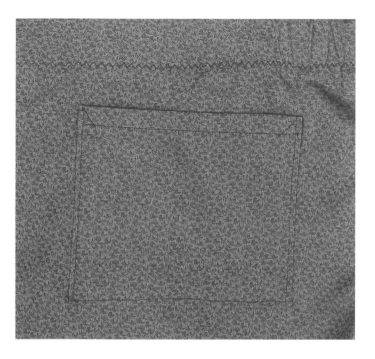

STEP 9
Finish the waist edge of the shorts with a zigzag or overlock stitch. Turn under ¼ in. (6 mm) and press.

STEP 10 ▶
Cut elastic to fit the waist measurement less 1 in. (25 mm). Overlap ends and stitch through both layers to secure.

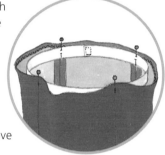

STEP 11 ▶
Mark the quarter points on both the elastic and waist edge of the shorts. Working from the wrong side of the shorts and with the elastic joined at the center back seam, pin baste the elastic and fabric together at the quarter points so that approximately ⅛ in. (3 mm) of the fabric is above the elastic.

STEP 12 ▶
Set the sewing machine to a small zigzag stitch and with the elastic stretched to the next point, machine stitch it in place as you stretch. You will need a hand at both sides of the presser foot as you sew and stretch. Progress from each quarter mark to the next. Repeat the process along the lower edge of the elastic.

STEP 13
Turn the elasticized waist to the wrong side, encasing the elastic, and pin baste again at the quarter marks. Working from the right side, zigzag stitch and stretch again along the lower edge of the elastic.

STEP 14
Turn up the hem 1 in. (25 mm), press, and fold under the raw edge ¼ in. (6 mm). Machine stitch close to the inner pressed edge.

TIPS: *Add a decorative trim to the hem edge or motifs to the patch pocket before stitching them to the garment.*
Cut each leg in a different color or pattern for a fun look.

SEAM FINISHES AND EDGES

While basic seam finishes are given on page 43, there are also many other finishes for use when seaming sheer or stretchy fabrics, for example, or when decorative seaming is required.

All seams are stitched on the seam line—also known as the stitching line. The distance from this line to the fabric edge is the seam allowance: usually ⁵/₈ in. (15 mm) on dressmaking projects and ¹/₄ in. (6 mm) on craft projects.

TIP: *Using an extra-wide seam allowance on fine material and pile fabrics makes it much easier to guide the fabric.*

DIRECTIONAL STITCHING

Stitching in the same direction as the fabric grain helps to prevent knitted and napped fabrics from stretching out of shape or curling. In fact, it is preferable to use directional sewing on all seams whenever possible.

CROSSING SEAMS

When seams cross—side seams crossed by a waistband, for example—there are two rules to bear in mind:

1 Always press a seam before another seam crosses it.

2 ▶ Trim the first seam allowance diagonally at the ends to reduce bulk within the seam allowance.

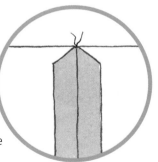

BIAS SEAMS

Because fabrics cut on the bias stretch more easily, seams need greater care. To prevent the seams from rippling, hold the fabric in front of and behind the presser foot, stretching it slightly as you stitch. The stitching will then relax into a smooth seam once it is carefully pressed.

▶ A bias seam stitched to a heavier-weight fabric might also need stabilizing to prevent drooping. Add a length of seam tape to the seam line and stitch through all layers.

KNIT SEAMS

▶▼ Knitted fabrics, such as jerseys, often need to be able to stretch, so it is necessary to stitch them with a flexible seam to prevent the stitches from breaking when the fabric stretches. Many machines have a range of stretch stitches to match the stretchiness of various fabrics. Alternatively, stitch with a zigzag stitch, stretching the fabric slightly as you sew.

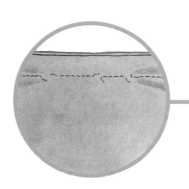

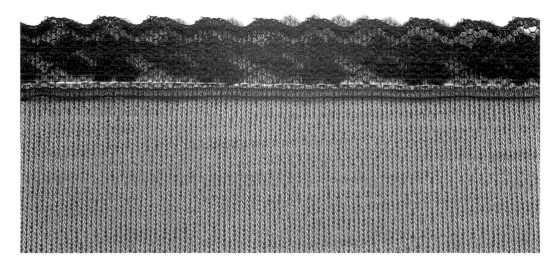

On areas of jerseys that need to keep their shape, such as shoulders and necklines, seams must be stabilized to prevent too much give

1 ◀ With right sides together, stitch a plain seam, with seam binding, ribbon, or twill tape along the seam line.

CORNERS

To strengthen seams at corners:

1 Reduce the stitch length along 1 in. (25 mm) of the seam before and after the corner.

2 ▶ Before turning through to the right side, trim the seam allowance of the outward corners diagonally.

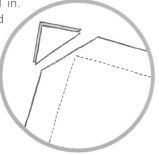

3 ▶ For sharp-angled corners, such as those on collars, take 1–2 diagonal stitches across the corner instead of stitching up to the point. Cut the corner off, as before, and trim diagonally on either side.

SPECIAL SEAMS

Some fabrics need special seaming techniques to give a professional-looking result. Where both sides of the fabric are visible—on unlined curtains, for example—or with sheer fabrics where seams show through, special seams are required.

DOUBLE-STITCHED SEAM

▶ Particularly useful for sheer clothing fabrics, this seam consists of two parallel rows stitched close together and then trimmed.

1 Use a straight stitch to stitch the seam on the seam line.

2 Stitch again, a scant ⅛ in. (3 mm) from the first line, using either a straight stitch or a small zigzag stitch.

3 Trim close to the stitching. Press to set the stitches and then press to one side.

FRENCH SEAM

◀ This neat seam looks good from back and front, and is perfect for unlined curtains and shades, and for garments of silk and similar fabrics.

1 With the wrong sides together, stitch a ⅜-in. (1-cm) seam.

2 Trim the seam allowance to a scant ⅛ in. (3 mm). Press.

3 Refold the fabric with right sides together, and with the stitched line on the fold, and press again.

4 ◀ Machine stitch ¼ in. (6 mm) from the fold, encasing the raw edges.

TOP-STITCHED SEAM

This is a plain seam finished with top stitching, which holds the seam allowances in place. It is especially useful for crease-resistant or heavyweight fabrics.

1 Stitch a plain seam.

2 Press seam allowances open. (If the fabric unravels easily, overcast seam allowances before pressing open.)

3 Top stitch on both sides of the seam, ¼ in. (6 mm) from the seam line.

4 For finer fabrics, press seam allowances to one side and top stitch in place through all layers.

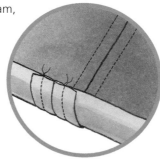

LAPPED SEAM

▶ A lapped seam leaves an unfinished edge showing and is therefore used on fabrics that don't fray, such as synthetic suede and leather.

1 Trim away the seam allowance on the top layer of fabric, which will overlap the underlayer.

2 Lap the fabric over the underlayer, placing the trimmed edge along the seam line of the underlayer. (If pins will leave holes, use double-sided basting tape to secure layers.)

3 Edge stitch close to the trimmed edge.

4 ▶ Top stitch ¼ in. (6 mm) from the first row of stitching, catching the seam allowance of the underlayer.

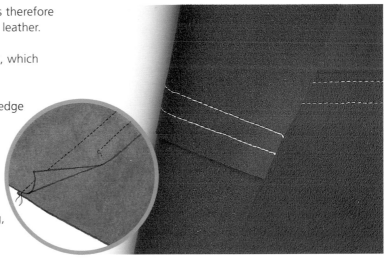

WELT AND DOUBLE-WELT SEAMS

◀ Similar to the top-stitched seam, these are particularly suitable for bulky fabrics. A double-welt seam is a welt with an additional row of edge stitching close to the seam line.

1 Stitch a plain seam and press seam allowances to one side.

2 ▶ Trim the under-seam allowance to ¼ in. (6 mm).

3 Working from the right side, top stitch ¼ in. (6 mm) from the seam, catching the untrimmed seam allowance.

FLAT FELL SEAM

▶ In a flat fell seam, the seam allowance is sewn on the right side of the fabric. This type of seam is often used on sportswear and reversible garments.

1 Stitch a plain seam with wrong sides together. Press seam allowances to one side.

2 Trim the under-seam allowance to a scant ⅛ in. (3 mm).

3 ▶ Turn the upper-seam allowance under ¼ in. (6 mm) and baste in place.

4 Edge stitch close to the fold.

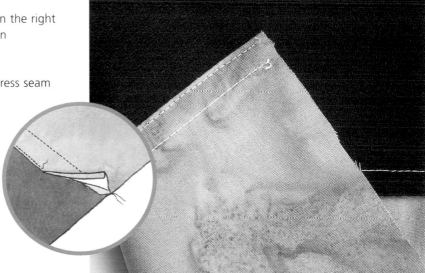

Dreamy Windows

Give your windows a treat with a new pair of dreamy voile curtains. Let them blow gently in the breeze, or swirl on the floor for a luxurious finish.

Voile curtains provide some privacy while allowing a lovely diffused light to enter the room. They are the "new lace curtains"— and a much softer option.

You will need
- Voile fabric, 3 x window width and length, plus allowances (see Measurements, below)
- Header tape (length needed is 3 x window width, plus allowances)
- Hem weight tape (as above)
- Toggle to secure pull cords
- Curtain hooks
- Polyester-covered sewing thread

Equipment
- Scissors and pins
- Weights (tin food cans could be used)
- Sewing machine

Measurements

To determine your fabric requirements, first measure the window area. Measure width from the outside edges of the curtain track, and length from the top of the track to the sill, radiator, or floor. To the length, add allowances, as follows:

Length
- Add height of header tape (if in doubt, add 4 in./10 cm).
- Add 4–8 in. (10–20 cm) for hems (large curtains look better balanced with bigger hems).
- Add the pattern repeat depth.

TIP: *For large windows, an additional fabric allowance is needed for seams and side turnings. For a small window, the seaming is minimal and no extra allowance is required.*

Example

This window is 40 in. wide x 54 in. high (102 x 137 cm). I used fabric 54 in. (137 cm) wide.

For a window 54 in. high, add 54 + 4 in. (for the header) + 4 in. (for the hems) = 62 in. length (137 + 10 + 10 cm = 157 cm).

To this total add any extra length necessary to match the pattern (see Fabric requirements, below). The number of lengths needed will depend on the total width required.

WIDTH

The total width depends upon two factors: the width of the chosen fabric and the fullness required. Lightweight voiles should be at least 3 x the width in fullness.

For a window 40 in. (102 cm) wide, you need a curtain width of 120 in. (306 cm)—3 x the window width. To achieve this, you will have to sew together at least 2¼ lengths of the 54-in. (137-cm) wide fabric, so buy three lengths and cut one to size. If the part-width is less than one-half, round the amount down to a full width; if more than one-half, round the amount up. The total width will be divided into two curtains.

FABRIC REQUIREMENTS

Calculate the fabric requirements as follows:
Length 62 in. + pattern repeat of 25 in.
= 87 in. per length x 3 widths = 261 in., or 7¼ yd.
(157 + 64 cm = 221 cm per length x 3 widths
= 663 cm, or 6.63 m).

TIP: *For fabric curtains, a good fullness is achieved by 2½ x window width.*

TIP: *Instead of cutting a length of voile into a smaller piece and wasting fabric, use it as a full width—voiles are so lightweight that extra material will not add excess bulk.*

TIP: *Choose an all-over pattern or a plain fabric to avoid buying extra material to match pattern repeats.*

STEP 1 ▶ Cut the number of fabric widths required to the correct length—in this example, it is 62 in. (157 cm). To make sure the pattern repeats line up across the width, follow these steps:

- Have the print facing up. If necessary, square the top edge and then cut the first length.
- Place this panel over the remaining fabric, the wrong side of the first panel on top of the right side of the remaining fabric. Match the pattern. Anchor In place with sewing weights or tin cans.
- Cut along the top and bottom edges, using the first panel as a guide. Repeat for the number of panels required.

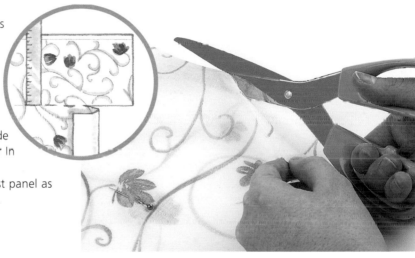

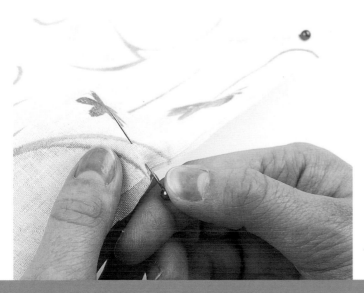

STEP 2 ▲ To make the two curtains in this example from three lengths, you need 1½ widths per curtain. To cut one panel into two equal pieces, fold the panel in half lengthwise. Pin at intervals through both thicknesses to hold it in place or anchor it with weights. Cut along the fold.

If one length needs to be a part-width, measure from one selvage and mark at intervals down the length. Cut off the excess (keep for test stitching).

STEP 3 ◀ Make French seams on voiles, since the wrong side will show through. To make the seam, with wrong sides together, pin a half panel to a full panel along one edge. Machine stitch ¼ in. (6 mm) from the edge, working from bottom to top.

TIP: *If the selvage edges are tight and appear to pucker, cut them off before pinning and stitching the seams. Alternatively, clip into the selvage diagonally in order to prevent puckering.*

TIP: *Work from bottom to top. That way, if the pattern begins to lose its match, the problem area will fall within the header and thus be less noticeable.*

STEP 4 ▶ Trim the seam allowance to a scant ⅛ in. (3 mm). Refold the fabric with right sides together and pin to encase raw edges. Machine stitch, in the same direction as before. Press. Repeat for all panels to be joined.

HEADER

STEP 5 Place the fabric on a flat surface, wrong side up. Turn the top edge over ½ in. (13 mm) and again 2½ in. (6 cm). If using a header tape wider or narrower than 2½ in., make the second fold the width of the curtain header tape plus ½ in. (13 mm). Press.

STEP 6 ▲ Pin the header tape, through all thicknesses, over the turned hem, starting approximately ½ in. (13 mm) from the top edge and 1 in. (25 mm) in from the side edges. Pin along both long edges.

STEP 7 Starting at the bottom corner of one side, stitch up and along the top edge of the tape. Repeat for the bottom edge, stitching in the same direction and then up the remaining side edge. Press.

HEM

STEP 8 ▲ Turn up a double hem at the bottom. Lay the fabric, wrong side up, on a large flat surface. Press the lower edge up 2 in. (5 cm) and then again 2 in. (5 cm) to form a double hem. Top stitch the hem by machine.

STEP 9 ▶ Add curtain weight tape by threading it through the hem channel. Hand stitch the ends to the hem allowance on the wrong side to secure.

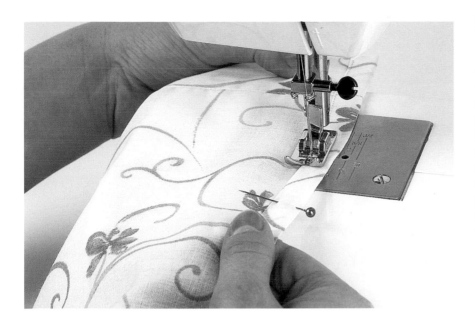

SIDE EDGES

STEP 10 ◄
Finish side edges by folding under 1½ in. (4 cm), tucking the raw edge under to meet the first fold. Pin and then stitch into place, close to the inner fold. Take care to encase raw header edges, but keep pull cords free on the outside edge (stitch over them to secure in place on the center edge of the curtain). Stitch from bottom to top of the curtain on both sides.

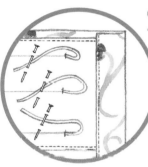

STEP 11 ◄
Gather the curtains to the correct fullness by dividing the window width into two: 40 in. ÷ 2 = 20 in. (102 cm = 51 cm). Pull up the header tape cords to gather the top, easing in the fullness until the width of each curtain is 20 in. (51 cm).

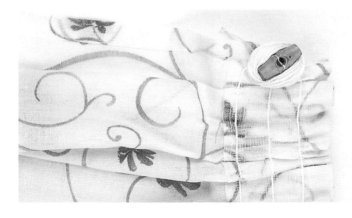

STEP 12 ▲
Add a small toggle to the side edge of the header tape to keep the pull cords neat.

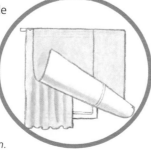

TIP: ► *Place part-panels at the edges so that the main expanse is seamless when the curtains are drawn.*

1 curtain = 1½ widths of fabric   1 curtain = 1½ widths of fabric

LARGE WINDOWS

Extra fabric is needed in the width to allow for seam allowances of ⅝ in. (15 mm) and side hems of 1½ in. (4 cm). To calculate this extra requirement, draw the number of panels needed and add up the total of seam allowances and side hems.

Example

Four panels require six seam allowances of ⅝ in. (15 mm) = 3¾ in. (10 cm) [one on left panel, two each on two center panels, and one on right panel] + two side hems of 1½ in. (4 cm) = 3 in. (8 cm) [one on left panel and one on right panel]. Total measurement for seam allowances and hems = 6¾ in. (18 cm).

Heavy furnishing fabrics and lined drapes should be hung for at least 24 hours before hemming. Finish side seams and the header, then gather and hang, allowing curtains to drop to their natural position. Cut edges evenly and hem as before.

PIPING

Piping adds a crisp decorative edge to soft furnishings, crafts, and fashions. Sewn within the seam, it creates a professional finish—and it is surprisingly easy to sew.

Piping is available in a variety of styles, colors, and widths. It usually comes attached to tape, which is sewn into the seam. You can make your own piping, using thin cord covered with bias strips of fabric. Other trims, such as beading or fringes, can be stitched in the same way as piping.

TIP: *Check that your chosen piping has the same wash care requirements as the main fabric.*

CHOOSING PIPING

▶ Piping can be plain, intricate, thick, or thin. For eye-catching edge treatment, choose a color that contrasts with the main fabric. For a subtle finish, select a coordinating trim. Bear in mind the weight of the fabric or the size of the cushion. For heavier furnishings, plump trims are preferable; for lightweight voiles or clothing, finer piping is more suitable.

Calculate the amount of trim needed by measuring the edges to be piped and adding ¹/₂ yd. (46 cm) for curves, corners, and overlapping ends.

STEPS TO SEW

Piping is added to the edges before seams are sewn together.

1 ▶ Pin trim to the right side of the main fabric of one section along the seam line. Position the piping/decorative edge toward the cushion center and the raw edge in the seam allowance.

2 Using a zipper foot, machine baste the trim in place along the seam line.

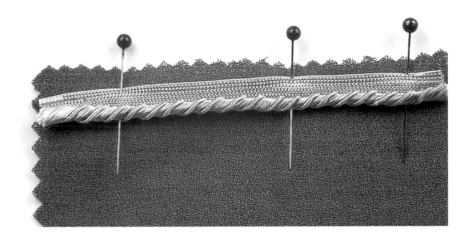

3 ◀▼ When piping shaped areas, curves, and corners, snip the tape at intervals to allow it to curve smoothly and lie flat.

OVERLAPPING ENDS

4 ▶ To join taped piping neatly, start by curving the first end from the edge onto the stitching line, as described above. Overlap ends by curving the top layer out to the seam allowance also. Make sure the overlapped ends are in the least conspicuous spot, such as the back of a cushion cover.

FINISHING

5 Pin the other main fabric section over the piped section, right sides together, matching edges.

6 Machine stitch, with piped section uppermost, close to the piping, so that all previous stitching is within the seam allowance.

7 Clip curves and corners, trim seam allowances, and turn through to the right side.

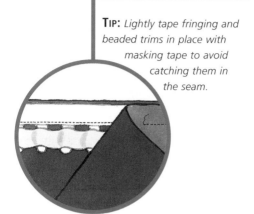

TIP: *Lightly tape fringing and beaded trims in place with masking tape to avoid catching them in the seam.*

MAKING YOUR OWN PIPING

The piping cover is made from bias strips of fabric (see Bias binding, pages 60–63). These can be from the main or a contrasting fabric. For cord that is up to ¼ in. (6 mm) thick, the strips need to be 1½ in. (4 cm) wide. For thicker cord, measure around the cord circumference and add 1 in. (25 mm) for seam allowances.

1 ◀ Fold the bias strip of fabric over the cord, with right side out and raw edges matching.

2 Using a zipper foot, machine baste close to the cord.

3 Apply piping to the main fabric section, as described above.

Joining ends

◄ Fabric-covered piping does not need to be overlapped. A neater finish can be achieved by joining the ends.

1 Place the piping so that the joined ends are in an inconspicuous place, such as the back of a cushion. (Avoid zipper ends, curves, or corners.)

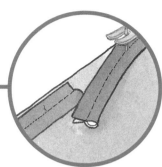

2◄ Pin one end of the piping at the marked point. Baste piping in place, starting 2 in. (5 cm) from the end and stopping 3 in. (8 cm) from the other end. Leave the needle down in the work.

3 Cut excess overlap piping, leaving a 1-in. (2.5-cm) tail.

4► Pull back the fabric cover on the overlap tail and trim the cord only, so that it will butt up to the other cording exactly.

5▼ Tuck the end of the overlap fabric cover under to encase the raw edges and then fold it back over the exposed cord and beginning of the piping.

6▼ Machine stitch to complete the stitching.

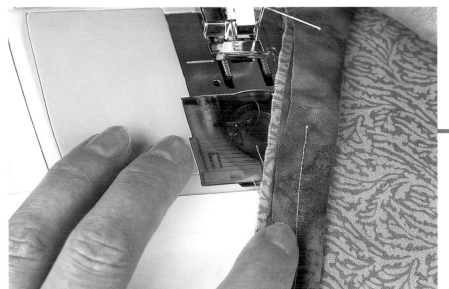

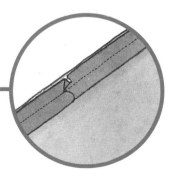

TRIMMED TIEBACKS

Create these attractive tiebacks with the aid of a little imagination and some stunning trims. The banana shape is easy to make and trim.

YOU WILL NEED
- ³⁄₄ yd. (69 cm) main fabric
- ¹⁄₂ yd. (46 cm) heavyweight iron-on interfacing
- 1¹⁄₂ yd. (138 cm) piping or beaded trim
- Four plastic rings, ¹⁄₂ in. (13 mm) in diameter
- Two cup hooks

EQUIPMENT
- Marker pen
- Sewing machine
- Scissors
- Zipper foot
- Embroidery scissors

place on fold line

Enlarge pattern by 400%

STEP 1 ◄ Enlarge this curved tieback pattern by the percentage given and cut out. Mark the fold line on the straight edge.

STEP 2 Fold the interfacing in half and pin the pattern through all thicknesses, matching the fold of the interfacing with the fold line on the pattern. Cut out. Repeat for the second tieback.

STEP 3 ▶ Fold the main fabric in half, right sides together. Put the pattern on the fabric, matching fold lines. Using a vanishing marker pen or chalk pencil, draw an outline ⁵⁄₈ in. (15 mm) outside the pattern for seam allowances. Cut along this line. Repeat until you have four fabric pieces (two for each tieback).

STEP 4 ▶ Position interfacing, adhesive side to wrong side of the front fabric piece. Using a steam iron set at silk/wool and a damp cloth, slowly press each area 5 or 6 times. Allow to cool. Repeat on the front of the second tieback.

STEP 5 ▼ From the right side of the interfaced section, pin beaded trim over the seam line so the tape edge is in line with the edge of the fabric, snipping tape at curves. Attach the zipper foot and stitch in place, ³/₈ in. (1 cm) from the edge.

STEP 6 ▶ Place the front and back pieces with right sides together, matching raw edges, and pin with the interfaced section uppermost, checking that beads do not catch in the seam line. With the zipper foot, stitch a scant ¹/₈ in. (3 mm) inside the first row of stitching, leaving a turning gap at the lower edge of about 6 in. (15 cm).

STEP 7 ▶ Trim the seam allowance to ¹/₄ in. (6 mm) around the stitching line, leaving all the seam allowance at the opening. Snip the allowance at the curves to allow the fabric to lie flat. Turn the tieback through to the right side and press.

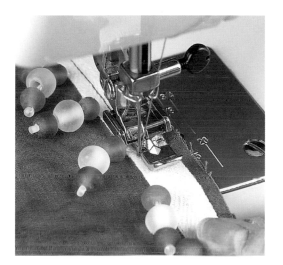

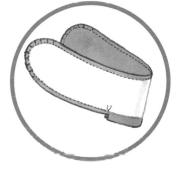

STEP 8 ◀ Fold in seam allowances on opening, press, and slip stitch in place.

STEP 9 ▶ Hand stitch tieback rings to the wrong side of the front half and the right side of the back half.

STEP 10 Attach cup hooks to the wall in line with the outside edge of the curtain, and loop the tieback around the curtain rings.

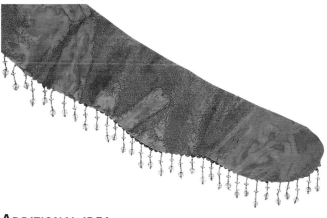

ADDITIONAL IDEA
Special tieback stiffener products are available, as well as patterns for three sizes and for scalloped tiebacks. These are very easy to use, although I suggest omitting a beaded or piped trim to the scalloped edge pattern until you are more confident with sewing curves and points.

DARTS

Darts are used to add shaping to garments, to mold the fabric to body contours, and to improve the fit. They can be placed at the sides, shoulders, or front for bust shaping, and at the center back and front for waist shaping.

The aim in making darts is to fold out excess fabric, tapering the fold to nothing within the garment, so that it provides gentle shaping. Darts can be single-ended or double-ended, where they widen in the middle and taper away at both ends. Occasionally, the dart stitching line is curved for a closer fit.

STEPS TO SEW

▶ Published patterns include dart placement and stitching lines on the pattern tissue. These must be transferred to the wrong side of the fabric sections, using tailor's tacks, tailor's chalk, or a marking pen.

◀ You may also need to make darts in simple wraparound skirts or pull-on tops for which there is no pattern. The dart length on skirts is the distance from waist to hip, and on tops, from side seam to mid-bust point.

When including darts in a simple skirt, remember that the total excess fabric to be darted out must be divided by the number of darts: for example, two darts in the front and two in the back. If the excess—the difference between hip and waist measurement—is more than 6 in. (15 cm), increase the number of darts.

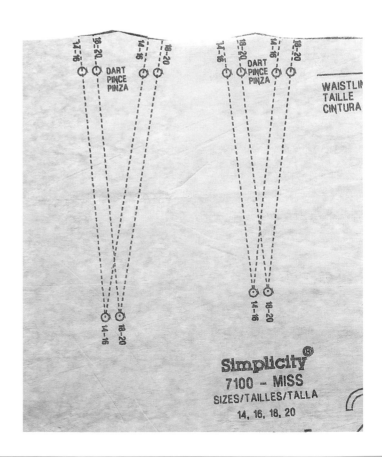

TIP: *Avoid having any dart larger than ³/₄ in. (2 cm) when folded at the widest point or it will be difficult to achieve a flat finish at the tapered end.*

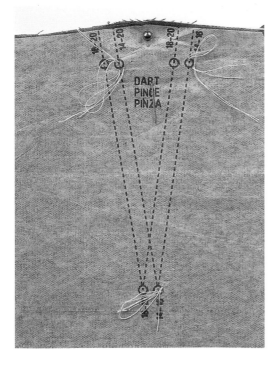

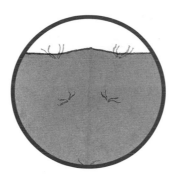

1. ◄ Mark the tip and two outer points of the darts, which will be folded together. For long darts, also mark areas on either side of the fold line.

2. With right sides together, fold the fabric at the dart, matching the marked points.

3. ◄ Pin the fabric layers together, tapering to nothing at the tip end.

4. ► Stitch from the widest end to the point, making the last few stitches exactly at the fold. Either fix the stitch or leave thread tails to knot—do not backstitch at the point, because this can cause a ridge.

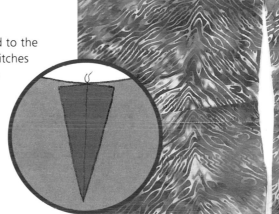
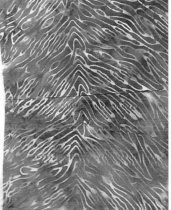

DOUBLE-ENDED DARTS

1. Stitch from the center point to one tapered end, as for a single dart. Repeat from the center to the other end. Again, fix the stitches at the ends or tie knots instead of backstitching.

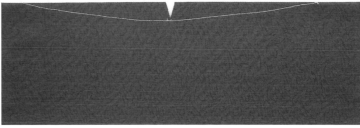

2. ► Clip the dart at the center (widest point), so that it will lie flat when pressed.

3. ◄ Press vertical darts toward the center and horizontal bust darts downward.

TIP: *When using heavy fabrics, such as wool or fleece, cut open the dart, snipping close to the tapered end, and press open. If the fabric frays easily, dab a spot of fray check at the tapered end.*

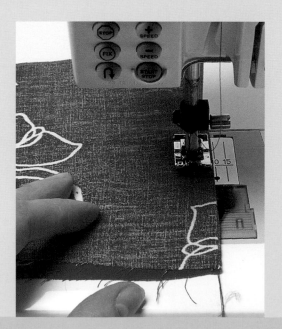

IT'S A WRAP

This is a great skirt design that is simple to make and suitable for a variety of fabrics. It is made from a rectangle of material, shaped by darts and hemming.

SIZE

Measure yourself to determine the size of rectangle needed.

A. Measure from your waist to the finished hem length (mid-calf or ankle). Add 2½ in. (6 cm) for hems.

B. Measure completely around your widest area: buttocks or hips. Add 1¼ in. (3 cm) for side hems.

C. Measure your front, hip to hip, for the front wrap panel. Again, add 1¼ in. (3 cm) for side hems.

Add measurements B and C together to determine the total width needed.

D. Measure around your waist (this measurement will be used later for adding darts).

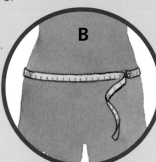

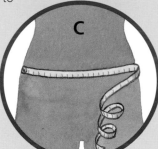

YOU WILL NEED

- Lightweight cotton fabric (for quantity, see the example below)
- Lightweight fusible interfacing or iron-on hem binding
- All-purpose sewing thread
- 2 buttons, diameter ½ in. (13 mm)

EQUIPMENT

- Marker pen
- Sewing machine
- Scissors

Example
Length: 30¾ + 2¼ in. for waist/hemming = 33 in. (78 + 6 cm = 84 cm)
Width B: 40 + 1¼ in. = 41¼ in. (102 + 3 cm = 105 cm)
Width C: 17¾ + 1¼ in. = 19 in. (45 + 3 cm = 48 cm)
Total width, B + C: = 60¼ in. (153 cm)

If your chosen fabric is wide enough, you can make the skirt from one panel. If it is less than the total width required, you will need to join panels.

STEP 1
Cut one length the width of measurement B. Cut a second length the width of measurement C.

STEP 2
▶ Using a French seam (see page 86), stitch two rectangles together. Press.

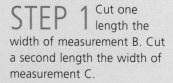

STEP 3
Shape the waist by adding four darts: two at the front, two at the back (the front two darts will be repeated in the wrap panel). To determine how much fabric to take in with the darts, deduct your waist measurement from your widest width measurement (B). Divide the remaining figure by four.

Example
Waist: 31½ in. (80 cm)
Widest measurement: 40 in. (102 cm)
Difference: 8½ in. (22 cm) ÷ 4 = 2⅛ in. (5.5 cm) each

STEP 4 Find the dart positions by wrapping the rectangle around your waist, starting at one side hip. Mark the center front and center back and the side without the seam (the seam should be positioned on one side).

STEP 5 ► Mark the dart positions an equal distance between center and side edges, two on the back and two on the front of the skirt section. Repeat two darts in the same position on the wrap section.

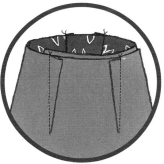

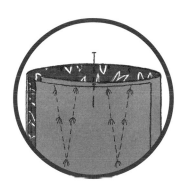

STEP 6 ◄ Make darts 8 in. (20 cm) long, each taking in the dart width determined in step 3 (in this example, 2⅛ in. or 5.5 cm) at the waist edge and tapering to nothing. Press darts to center back and center front.

STEP 7 ► Finish the raw edge of the waist by turning it under to the wrong side by ⅜ in. (1 cm). Using a zigzag stitch, machine stitch in place. Press.

STEP 8 ◄ Fold the waist edge under again, by ¾ in. (2 cm), and press. Then open the edge out, fuse a strip of iron-on interfacing or hem binding to the wrong side, and close it again. This gives a slight firmness at waist.

STEP 9 From the wrong side, using a straight stitch, machine stitch close to the zigzagged edge.

STEP 10 Double hem the raw side edge by turning it under ⅜ in. (1 cm) to the wrong side and then ⅜ in. (1 cm) again. Press. From the right side, top stitch in place. Repeat for the bottom edge.

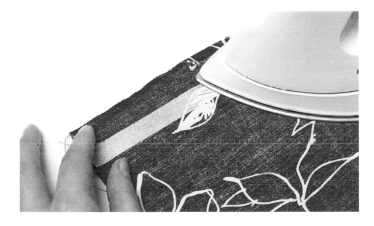

STEP 11 ► Make buttonholes in the waistband opposite the side with the seam. Make another in the side edge of the wrap. To finish, position buttons on the waistband to correspond to the buttonholes.

STEP 12 If your chosen button does not have a raised shank on the back, add a thread shank (see page 71).

TIP: *For crisp corners where the side edge meets the hem, turn the corners to the wrong side ¾ in. (2 cm) before double folding in the raw edges as above. The finished side and hem edges will then meet, making a neat mitered corner.*

ZIPPERS AND OTHER FASTENERS

Zippers can be inserted by centering or lapping. When they are centered, each side is stitched equally; when they are lapped, they are stitched unevenly so that one side of the fabric overlaps the other. Back zippers and zippers on bags are usually centered; those used as side fastenings or fly fronts are more often lapped.

CHOOSING A ZIPPER
The weight of the zipper should be appropriate to the weight of the fabric and the use it will get. For example, outdoor clothing needs hardwearing zippers—metal is more robust. For soft furnishings, lightweight zippers with plastic teeth are suitable. Jeans and pants may need metal zippers, whereas the invisible zipper is the most popular choice for dresses and skirts.

Choose a zipper that is ¹/₂–1 in. (13–25 mm) longer than the opening to be zipped. If you cannot find a zipper of the correct length, buy a longer one and shorten it. Make a hand-stitched bar tack at the end by stitching from side to side on the same spot 6–10 times, using a double strand of strong thread. Then simply cut off the excess.

CENTERED ZIPPERS
Centered zippers are placed with the teeth along the seam line and have stitching on either side, equidistant from the edge.

1 Machine stitch the seam line from the hem to the bottom of the zipper placement.

2 Continue stitching along the seam line, using basting stitches.

3 Finish seam allowances, with your chosen method, and press them open.

TIP: *Always stitch in the same direction on both sides, starting at the bottom of the zipper. This helps to prevent puckering.*

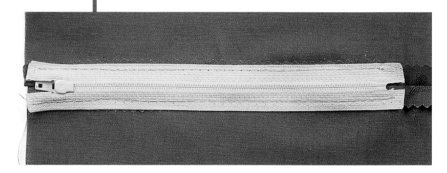

4 ▲ Place the zipper face down over the seam, with the teeth centered over the basting stitches. The top of the zipper should be within the seam allowance at the top of the garment. Baste in position.

5 ◄ Adjust the zipper foot and the needle position for each side, so that the foot and needle are to the right of the teeth when stitching the right side, and to the left of the teeth when stitching the left side.

6 Working from the right side of the fabric, machine stitch from the seam line at the bottom, just below the teeth and bottom "stop." Stitch across approximately ³/₈ in. (1 cm), with the needle down, then pivot the work to stitch straight up one side, keeping a scant ³/₈ in. (1 cm) from the teeth.

7 ▶ Stop approximately 2 in. (5 cm) from the top, with the needle down. Lift the presser foot and ease the slider down below the needle. You may have to snip the basting stitching that is holding the seam closed.

8 Continue stitching to the end, fixing the stitch or backstitching.

9 Repeat for the other side, again working from the bottom up.

10 Remove all the basting stitches.

TIPS: *Always use a zipper foot when inserting zippers. Move it to the right or left of the needle in order to stitch close to the teeth.*

To prevent the bump that often occurs when trying to stitch past the slider and pull tab, select a zipper that is 1–2 in. (25 mm–5 cm) longer than required and position it so that the excess is above the top placement. Machine stitch in place, cut off the excess, and use the facing/collar as a "stop."

SEPARATING (OPEN-ENDED) ZIPPERS

▶ Separating (open-ended) zippers are used on jacket-style garments and items such as bags. They come apart completely. To make sure the ends match evenly, baste garment fronts together along the seam line as for a centered zipper, finishing raw edges as before.

1 Place the zipper face down over the seam, centering teeth over the basted stitches. Baste into position.

2 At this point, you can remove the seam basting stitches, open the zipper, and work on each side separately.

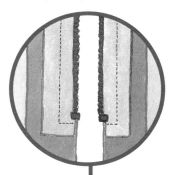

3 ◀ Again start from the bottom, fix the stitch, and machine stitch to the top, adjusting the zipper foot and needle position so that the stitching is a scant ³/₈ in. (1 cm) from the teeth.

TIP: *Use a heavier-weight needle for chunky zippers to help penetrate the thick zipper tape and garment fabric.*

4 ▶ If the garment has a facing, place the facing over the zipper and baste it in position. Machine stitch with the zipper foot close to the teeth, continuing around the neck and hem edges as applicable.

5 Clip the corners. Press, and turn the facing to the wrong side. Repeat for the second side, checking that the slider is moved out of the way of the machine needle. Top stitch through all thicknesses if desired.

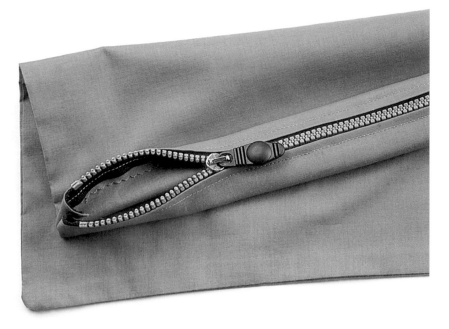

DECORATIVE SEPARATING ZIPPERS

◀ Sometimes zippers are used as decorative finishes and the teeth are meant to be visible. In that case, finish raw edges of the fabric as before, fold to the wrong side ⅝ in. (15 mm), and press.

1 Separate the zipper and, working with the zipper right side up, place the pressed folded edge of the fabric along the edge of the teeth. Baste in position.

2 Edge stitch close to the fold.

> **TIP:** *For easier handling, cut a larger-than-normal seam allowance of ¾ in. (2 cm) where the zipper will be placed.*

LAPPED ZIPPERS

▼ Lapped zippers are used in side fastenings and are similar to fly-front zippers.

> **TIP:** *Make sure that the top of the zipper is placed far enough down the seam to allow plenty of room for the facing, collar, waistband, and so on, to be sewn in place.*

1 Mark the zipper position and baste the zipper seam together, machine stitching the rest of the seam down to the hem, as before. Press the seam allowance open.

2 Open the zipper and place it face down. Pin and hand baste the zipper tape to the left seam allowance only.

3 Close the zipper and turn it face up. Fold the same seam allowance along the zipper teeth and, using a zipper foot, stitch as close to the folded edge as possible. Clip the seam allowance below the zipper end.

4 Spread the garment flat and hand baste the zipper through all thicknesses across the bottom and up the other side.

5 Working from the right side, again machine stitch using the zipper foot, starting at the bottom and working up to the top, removing pins as you stitch. This forms the lapped side. Remove the basting.

> **TIP:** *Place a piece of tape alongside the stitching line as a guide. This can be masking or quilter's tape.*

INVISIBLE ZIPPERS

▶ Invisible zippers are lightweight and come in basic colors. They are different from other zippers because the teeth cannot be seen from the right side—perfect if you are unsure how straight you can stitch! Invisible zippers are inserted before the seam is sewn and are stitched from top to bottom on both sides, instead of bottom to top, as with other zippers.

An invisible zipper foot, with deep grooves underneath for the zipper teeth, is needed for perfect results. If using a regular zipper foot, baste the zipper in place, then position the foot and adjust the needle position as close to the teeth as possible. Push the teeth to one side as you stitch, getting as close as you can to the teeth without catching them with the needle.

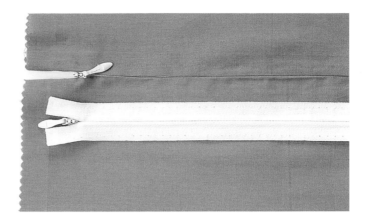

1 Allow ¾ in. (2 cm) extra seam allowance at the zipper placement area and at the top, for the waistband.

2 Turn over and press both sides of the seam allowance of the zipper area, and open out again. This will give you a straight line for guidance.

3 Place the open zipper face down on the seam allowance with teeth on the seam line. Baste it in place to the seam allowance only.

4 Use the invisible zipper foot. Starting at the top, sew the first side of the zipper in place, stitching so that the teeth are in the groove of the foot and the stitches are as close to the teeth as possible. Stitch to within ¾ in. (2 cm) of the lower end. Remove the basting and close the zipper.

5 Repeat for the second side, pin, and baste the remaining zipper tape to the seam allowance, as before.

6 Open the zipper and, again starting at the top, sew it in place, stitching to within ¾ in. (2 cm) of the lower end.

7◀ Pull the zipper tape end to one side. Pin and baste the remaining seam in place from the hem to the bottom of the zipper to join the zipper stitching exactly. Stitch, using the regular zipper foot. Make sure you do not catch the end of the zipper tape in the seam.

8 Finish by hand stitching the bottom of the zipper tape to the seam allowance to prevent the seam stitching from taking all the strain of the zipper pull when in use.

TIP: *When working with delicate fabric, add stability by applying edge tape or a strip of lightweight iron-on interfacing to the wrong side of the seam line where the zipper will be placed.*

TIP: *When covering buttons in lightweight fabric, use two layers of fabric, or add a layer of interfacing, to prevent the button from showing through.*

OTHER FASTENERS

▶ Some kinds of fastener are hand stitched; others are applied with special tools that clamp them into the fabric (instructions come with the tool). These are useful for projects with many closures, such as pillow covers, and as decorative trims for fashion clothes.

◀ Snaps and hooks and eyes come in various sizes, and are made from nickel, black metal, or clear plastic. Use the correct weight to suit the project and hand stitch in place with a double strand of matching thread, taking 2–3 stitches through each sewing hole. On clothing, place snaps with the "ball" side facing away from the body.

Also available are fabric-covered buttons. These are useful when you cannot find a perfect color match or size in a regular button. Supplied in different sizes, they come complete with instructions for covering.

GET SPORTY

Make your own sports bag, using the techniques you've just learned for inserting zippers and piping. This project looks impressive and will save you money!

The bag pictured here has been made with circular ends and a tubular design, but it is just as easy to work with squared ends. Piping on the ends and pocket tops provides a crisp, firm finish, but for speed and simplicity you could leave it out.

Diagram labels:

54"

23" (58 cm)

selvage — 36" (92 cm)

MAIN BODY

SIDE 12" (30 cm) sq

SIDE 12" (30 cm) sq

POCKET 1 12 x 7" (30 x 18 cm)

POCKET 1a 12 x 7" (30 x 18 cm)

POCKET 2 12 x 7" (30 x 18 cm)

POCKET 2a 12 x 7" (30 x 18 cm)

PIPING COVER 1¾ x 36" (4 x 92 cm)
PIPING COVER 1¾ x 36" (4 x 92 cm)
PIPING COVER 1¾ x 36" (4 x 92 cm)

STEP 1 ▲ Cut fabric pieces, following the diagram above, as follows:

- main body: 36 x 23 in. (92 x 58 cm)
- sides x two: 12 in. (30 cm) square
- pocket pieces x four: 12 x 7 in. (30 x 18 cm)
- strips for piping cover x three: 1¾ x 36 in. (4 x 92 cm), using contrasting fabric if preferred.

STEP 2 ◄ Place the side pieces right sides together and pin to hold. Using a dinner plate as a template, draw around the plate with a chalk pencil. Draw around again, ⅝ in. (15 mm) outside the first line, to create seam allowances. Cut out and separate the pieces.

STEP 3 ▲▶ Layer two pocket pieces, right sides together, and pin to hold. Use the dinner plate to draw a semicircle on the fabric. Again, add seam allowances, ⁵⁄₈ in. (15 mm) from the first line. Cut out. Repeat for the other pocket set.

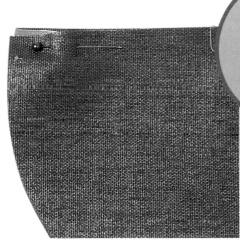

STEP 4 ◀ Cut two pieces of interfacing the same size as the pocket pieces, one for each set. Pin interfacing to the wrong side of one pocket piece and machine stitch ¼ in. (6 mm) from the edge.

STEP 5 ▲ Machine stitch piping strips together at the short ends to make one long piece. Fold this long strip in half lengthwise, wrong sides together, and press. Insert piping cord in the fold and, using the zipper foot, sew the edges together, encasing the cord.

STEP 6 ◀ Pin the covered piping between the straight edges of two pocket pieces (one interfaced, one plain), placed right sides together, matching raw edges. Cut off the excess piping and leave to one side. Using the zipper foot, machine stitch close to the piping cord. Repeat for the other pocket set. Turn through to the right side.

STEP 7 ▼ Pin the pocket section to the right side of the side section, matching circular edges. Repeat for the other side.

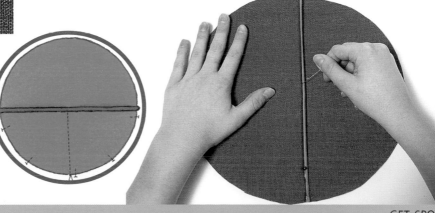

TIP: ▶ Divide one pocket into two, for carrying toiletries, by machine stitching through all thicknesses from the piping to the raw edges.

OPTIONAL

STEP 8 Add snaps or peel-apart fasteners to the pocket and corresponding side piece. If using snaps, iron a patch of interfacing to the wrong side of the side panel behind the fastener placement to strengthen it.

STEP 9 ◀ ▼ Pin piping to the right side of the circular side pieces, snipping the seam allowance of the piping fabric to fit curves. Machine or hand baste into position. Set this aside until the main body is ready.

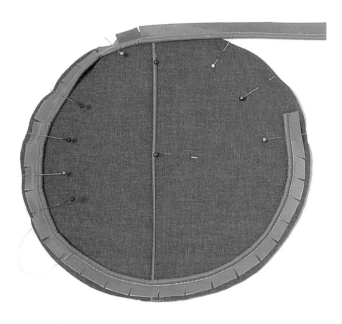

TIP: *Pin basting is done by placing pins at close intervals to hold the fabric and zipper tape together. If preferred, hand or machine baste to hold securely before machine stitching.*

INSERT ZIPPER

STEP 10 ◀ Working with the main piece of fabric, turn under the raw edges of the short ends by ½ in. (13 mm), and again by the same amount, so that the raw edge meets the fold. Pin baste the opened zipper to the wrong side of one edge, butting the fold of the fabric up against the zipper teeth, with the zipper 1½ in. (4 cm) from the raw ends. Working from the right side, machine stitch the zipper into position, close to the edge of the zipper teeth. Backstitch at the end to secure.

STEP 11 ▶ Close the zipper, then pin and stitch its other side to the other folded edge of the main fabric, as before. At the end of the zipper, stitch an X for added strength.

STEP 12 ▼ Cut the webbing into three pieces: a shoulder strap of 46 in. (117 cm) and two handles, each 22 in. (56 cm) long. Finish both ends of each piece by turning them under 1 in. (25 mm) and machine stitching a square around all edges.

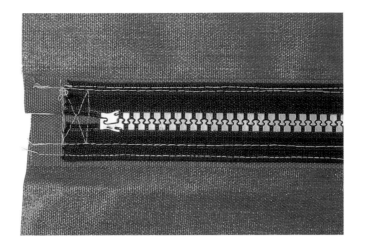

STEP 13 ▶ Find the center of the zipper section and mark the handle placement points, 4 in. (10 cm) on either side and 6 in. (15 cm) below the zipper teeth. Pin the handles to the main fabric, with the wrong side of the handle to the right side of the fabric, over the placement lines.

STEP 14 ▼ Machine stitch into position, close to the edge of the webbing, across the bottom, up 2 in. (5 cm), and across and down 2 in. (5 cm) to join the start of the stitching.

STEP 15 Baste the bag seam allowances together at both zipper ends. Pin the ends of the shoulder strap to the right side of the main body, centering over the basted zipper ends. Work a square of machine stitching as before to hold them securely.

STEP 16 ▶ Turn the bag section so that the right side is inside and pin it to the side panels, again with right sides in. Pin all around, through all thicknesses (side panel, piping tape, main fabric, webbing ends, and pocket set). Machine or hand baste, checking that only the ends of the shoulder strap are stitched. Working slowly, stitch all around, stopping with the needle down and pivoting the work slightly to maintain shaping.

STEP 17 Clip seam allowances and finish the edges with bias binding or overstitching.

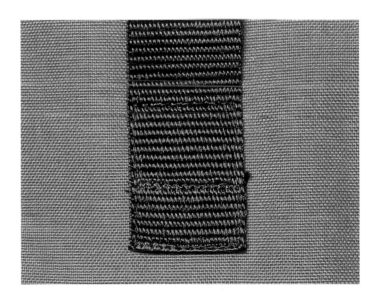

TIP: *Check that the zipper is open before stitching the second side panel to the bag, so that it can be turned through when finished.*

APPLIQUÉ

Appliqué is the technique of stitching a fabric cutout onto a main fabric base—usually to create a design. Use it to brighten plain items, such as cushions and children's clothes. Buy ready-made appliqué designs or make your own.

The design can be a simple shape or a motif to match your project, cut from plain or printed fabric. Appliqués are usually stitched with a narrow zigzag or satin stitch, or with a blanket stitch if the appliqué fabric does not unravel easily.

Secure the appliqué to the main fabric before stitching, using either a light application of fabric glue or double-sided fusible bonding.

If available, use a satin stitch presser foot when stitching appliqué. It has a groove in the bottom that glides over the raised concentrated stitches.

PLAIN APPLIQUÉ

▼ This is the usual method of stitching motifs and picture designs to clothes and furnishings.

1 Cut the paper-backed fusible bonding roughly to size and fuse in place to the wrong side of the appliqué. Once cool, cut out the appliqué accurately.

2 Determine the position of the appliqué on the main fabric, remove the paper backing from the bonding, and fuse in place. Allow to cool completely before stitching.

1 Set your sewing machine to a short stitch length and narrow- to medium-width zigzag stitch.

2 Position the work so that the appliqué is just to the left of the needle when the needle is in the right-hand swing of the zigzag stitch.

3 Stitch slowly to control direction and to be sure of achieving smooth edges.

TIP: *When adding appliqué to lightweight fabrics, place a layer of tear away interfacing underneath the area being stitched. This will prevent the flimsy fabric from being pulled into the feed dogs of the machine by the heavy concentration of stitching.*

HANDLING CURVES

▶ For outside curves, stop with the needle in the right-hand position, so that it is in the main fabric. Lift the presser foot and pivot the fabric slightly. Lower the presser foot and continue stitching.

For inside curves, stop with the needle in the left-hand position, so that it is in the appliqué. Raise the presser foot, pivot the fabric, lower the presser foot, and continue.

RAW EDGE APPLIQUÉ

▼ This "country-look" appliqué method is quick and easy to sew. It is perfect for beginners, and fun for children to try. The edges of the appliquéd design are left raw. It is wise, therefore, to use a fabric that does not fray too easily. Cotton and calico are both good choices. An alternative is to clip the edges with pinking shears to minimize fraying.

1 Cut out the design, adding a ½-in. (13-mm) seam allowance.

2 Straight machine stitch around the motif, ½ in. (13 mm) from the edge, using matching or contrasting thread (depending on the look you want to achieve).

3 ◀ Apply double-sided fusible bonding to the reverse of the appliqué, keeping within the stitched area.

4 When the position is right, fuse the appliqué to the main fabric, as before.

5 Again using a straight stitch, machine stitch the motif to the main fabric, following the previous stitching lines or stitching ⅛ in. (3 mm) from the first row of stitching.

ADDITIONAL IDEAS

▶ Create a raised appearance by sandwiching a layer of batting between the appliqué and the main fabric. Hand baste the appliqué in position to secure it before machine stitching as before.

Use different fabrics, such as fake fur for animals or lace for dresses, to add interesting textural detail.

MITERING

Sooner or later, when adding trims and finishes, corners will be involved. To achieve a crisp, professional look, the fabric needs to be mitered. This technique is especially useful for patch pockets, placemat borders, and the slit hems of skirts.

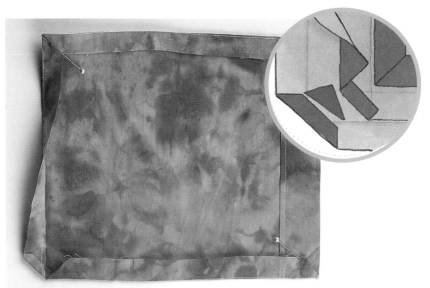

TIP: *To keep the corners in place when top stitching or edge stitching a pocket to the main garment, slip stitch the corners together on the wrong side.*

MITERING TRIMS

▶ Every time a trim turns a corner, it needs to be mitered.

FLAT TRIMS

1 Pin the trim in place and top stitch both edges, ending stitching when the corner is reached.

2 Fold the trim back upon itself and press. Holding the fold, again fold the trim diagonally so that it is at right angles and the edge is along the placement line. Press.

3 ▶ Undo the second fold so that the trim is just folded back on itself, and stitch along the diagonal fold through all layers.

4 Turn the trim back along the diagonal line of stitching and press. Continue top stitching both edges.

FOLDED MITER

◀ Use this method for patch pockets and slit hems.

1 Stitch along the pocket seam lines and then press seam allowances along the stitching line, folding in toward the pocket.

2 Open out the seam allowance at the corners. Fold up diagonally and press again. Trim this diagonal fold to ¼ in. (6 mm).

3 Fold all seam allowances back to the inside again. The folded edges will just meet at the corners, forming a nice miter.

FANCY TRIMS

The method of mitering is basically the same for fancy trims. However, these trims are usually positioned on the edge, with the fancy edging hanging free. It may be necessary to fold and refold the diagonal corner until the trim lies neatly.

Hats Off!

Make a scarf and hat set quickly and easily, using appliqué and zigzag stitching. It couldn't be simpler!

STEP 1 Cut fleece for the hat, 23¹/₂ x 11³/₄ in. (60 x 30 cm).

STEP 2 Cut fleece for the scarf, 60 x 10 in. (152 x 25 cm). For a child, reduce the length as desired.

STEP 3 Iron on paper-backed fusible bonding to the wrong side of the orange and blue fabric remnants. Once the bonding has cooled, cut out small (1-in./25-mm-sided), medium (1½-in./4-cm-sided), and large (2-in./5-cm-sided) triangles to decorate the hat and scarf:

Orange Hat: 1 x small, 3 x medium; Scarf: 1 x medium, 3 x large

Blue Hat: 2 x small, 1 x medium; Scarf: 2 x medium, 1 x large

Hat

STEP 4 ▶ Fold the hat piece in half, right sides together, so that it is 11³/₄ in. (30 cm) square. Pin mark 3 in. (8 cm) in from the bottom and top edges on the fold and again 4 in. (10 cm) in from the sides along the top edge. These marks indicate the brim depth and the curve depth at the top.

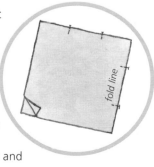

STEP 5
Cut a convex curve from the top pin mark at the fold to the nearest pin mark on the top edge. Fold the fabric in half again (so that there are four layers) and cut out the corresponding curve on the other side.

STEP 6
▶ Open out the fabric completely, and transfer the brim pin mark to the front of the fabric. Arrange the triangles in the center of one side (which will be the front of the hat). Turn up the brim at the pin mark, tucking the raw edge under ½ in. (13 mm), and position the brim triangle. When you are satisfied with the positioning, carefully peel away the paper backing from the triangles and fuse them in place, using a press cloth and hot iron. Leave to cool.

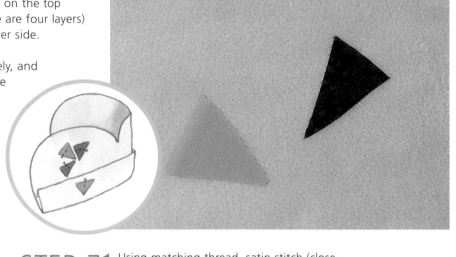

STEP 7
◀ Using matching thread, satin stitch (close zigzag stitch) around the edge of each triangle. Work slowly, stopping at each corner with the needle in the work. Raise the presser foot, pivot the fabric, lower the presser foot, and continue. Stitch all the orange triangles and then change needle thread to stitch all the blue triangles. Note that the brim triangle is stitched to the wrong side of the fabric, so that it will appear on the right side when the brim is turned up.

STEP 8
▶ Using a chalk pencil, draw swirls onto tear away stabilizer. Position on the right side of the hat fabric as desired, pin in place, and then satin stitch over the chalk curves. Remember that the brim swirl must be stitched onto the wrong side of the fabric, so that it is on the right side when the brim is turned up. Again, stitch slowly, pivoting at curves with the needle down in the outer area of the curve. Tear away the stabilizer and carefully press the appliqués, using a press cloth (or fleece remnant as a press cloth) to protect the pile.

STEP 9 ► With wrong sides together, fold the hat in half and sew together the side seam from the bottom up to the 3-in. (8-cm) brim pin mark. Clip the seam allowance at right angles, just below the end of the stitching.

STEP 10 Turn the hat through so the right sides are together, and stitch the rest of the side seam, all around the curved top.

TIP: *When sewing two or more layers of fleece, use a larger-than-normal stitch length.*

STEP 11 Fold the hat in half lengthwise and find the center of the curved seam at the top. Pin mark this point, then unfold the hat and pin a double dart at right angles to the curved seam. Take ½ in. (13 mm) at the dart center, tapering to nothing approximately 4 in. (10 cm) in both directions, so that the total dart length is 8 in. (20 cm). Machine stitch, working from the center to the end on both sides.

STEP 12 Clip the seam allowance of the curved seam. Press carefully. Turn the hat through to the right side.

STEP 13 Turn up the raw edges of the hat brim ½ in. (13 mm) to the right side, and blind hem in place. Press carefully. Turn the brim up at the brim pin mark, and gently press in place.

TIP: *When sewing small sections or hems on circular items such as this hat, convert your sewing machine to free arm by removing the flat-bed section.*

SCARF

STEP 1 Appliqué triangles and satin stitch swirls to the right side of both ends of the scarf, positioning as desired. Fuse and stitch following steps 6–8 above. Press gently, using a spare fleece remnant as a press cloth.

STEP 2 ◄ Cut off the corners at each end to reduce bulk and then fold under the raw edges ½ in. (13 mm) along the short ends and side edges. The corners should meet at a neat angle.

STEP 3 ▲ Using a wide zigzag stitch, top stitch the folded edges in place, stitching ⅝ in. (15 mm) from the edge. If necessary, slip stitch the corner edges together on the wrong side.

WAISTBANDS, COLLARS, CUFFS, AND FACINGS

Waistbands, collars, cuffs, and facings are the tops and tails of dressmaking. As with all basic dressmaking techniques, there are some simple steps to success.

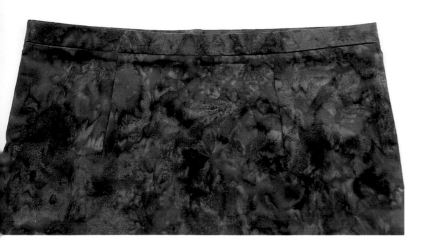

INTERFACING

The first step is to interface the wrong side of the waistband, collar, cuff, or facing. Choose an interfacing that provides the body or stiffness required. For cottons, polyester cottons, and wool blends, an iron-on interfacing is best. For knits and stretch fabrics, a stretch sew-in interfacing is preferable.

MATCHING PIECES

Dressmaking patterns have notches in the pattern pieces for the waistbands, collars, and cuffs that correspond with notches in the main body of the garment. These are matched up for a perfect fit. If making a garment without a pattern, match front or ends and center back with the center of the collar, waistband, or cuff. Then pin the rest of the garment to the collar, easing in fullness as required.

WAISTBANDS

To fit comfortably, waistbands should be approximately 1/2–1 in. (13 mm–25 mm) larger than the actual waist size. One end of the waistband will also overlap the other (this lapped section has the buttonhole). Allow approximately 1 1/4 in. (3 cm) for the overlap.

To eliminate bulk in waistband seams, cut the waistband on the selvage so that it does not need finishing, or overcast one straight edge, reducing the seam allowance by 1/4 in. (6 mm).

Interface half the waistband with a specific waistband product, such as nonwoven stiffener, or the entire waistband (excluding seam allowances), using an appropriate weight interfacing (light, medium, or heavy to suit the fabric).

1 ▶ With right sides together, attach the notched edge of the interfaced waistband to the garment, matching notches and markings. Machine stitch, trim seam allowances, and press the seam toward the waistband.

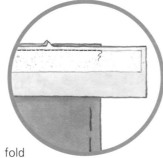

2 ◀ Next, fold the waistband over, right sides together, and stitch the overlap end, pivoting at the corner. Clip close to the garment edge.

3 Turn the waistband to the right side along the fold line so that the selvage edge overlaps the waistband seam on the inside. Press.

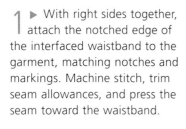

4 ◀ Working from the right side, pin the waistband layers together along the waistline seam.

5 ▶ Again working on the outside, stitch in the ditch, or groove, of the waistband seam, catching the finished edge of the waistband on the inside as you go.

COLLARS

A collar has two visible layers, the top and the underlayer, which may also be the facing. Sandwiched between is the interfacing. Occasionally, the top and underlayer are made from one piece folded in two.

There are three main types of collar: flat, rolled, and standing. The flat collar lies flat against the neck edge. The rolled collar rises straight up and then rolls down to rest on the garment. The standing collar is a band that rises straight up. Your chosen pattern will cover attaching a particular collar style, but there are some basic steps that affect all collar types.

FACINGS AND BANDS

Often part of a collar, facings or bands can also be used in place of collars and cuffs. They can be cut from the same fabric as the main body of the garment or from a lighter-weight fabric.

Facings are interfaced in the same manner as collars and cuffs, whereas bands need interfacing applied to half the length only.

Finish the outside edge of facings and bands before attaching them to the garment by turning the raw edge under and top stitching or overcasting/serging the raw edge.

Attach facings and bands to the main garment in the same way as waistbands, collars, and cuffs, matching markings or notches, and grading and clipping seam allowances.

When the seam between the facing and the main garment should sit on the fold, roll it between fingers and thumb so that the stitching line falls just to the inside edge.

1 In most cases, the interfacing is attached to the upper collar section.

2 To reduce bulk, eliminate the seam allowances on fusible interfacings or trim close to the stitching on sew-in interfacings.

3 To achieve sharp corners or curves, reduce the stitch length just before and after the corner, and take one stitch diagonally across the point. Trim interfacing diagonally at corners within the stitching line.

4 When stitching collar sections together, begin in the center and work to each end instead of starting at an end. This gives a more symmetrical finish.

5 Trim and grade the seam allowances, and notch and clip curves.

6 Before turning the collar through, press it on both sides to fix the stitches, pressing the seam allowances open.

7 ◄ Turn through and ease the corners out, using a point turner.

CUFFS

Cuffs are often made of three layers: top, underlayer (also known as the facing), and interfacing, which is sandwiched in between. Sometimes the upper and underlayers are cut from one piece of fabric, folded in two.

Cuffs can be one continuous band or have an opening. If there is an opening, there will be a corresponding sleeve finish. Your pattern will provide step-by-step instructions. Cuffs can be treated in much the same way as waistbands and collars.

UNDERSTITCHING

Understitching is a row of stitching used to prevent the inside layers, usually the facings, from rolling to the outside.

1 ► Trim seam allowances, grade, clip, and notch, then press seam allowances toward the facing.

2 On the right side of the garment, stitch ⅛ in. (3 mm) from the seam line, through the facing and seam allowances only.

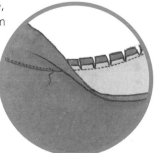

Kimono Comfort

Made in cotton, silk, or warm fleece, this is an easy design that suits all sizes and both sexes.

This kimono is ankle length, but it could be knee or thigh length, if preferred.

You will need

Adult size
- 3¼ yd. of 45-in.-wide fabric (3 m of 114 cm width)
- ½ yd. (46 cm) fusible interfacing
- Matching all-purpose sewing thread

Equipment
- Loop turner
- Sewing machine
- Scissors

Preparing Fabric

STEP 1 The front and back of the garment are cut as one piece. Calculate the length needed, as follows:
- For ankle length, measure height from the nape of the neck to the ankle and double this figure. Add another 4½ in. (12 cm) for seam allowance and hems.

Example: Nape of neck to ankle 54 in. x 2 = 108 in. + 4½ in. = 112½ in. (137 cm x 2 = 274 cm + 12 cm = 286 cm).

- For knee length, measure height from the nape of the neck to the knee and double this figure. Add 4½ in. (12 cm) for seam allowance and hems.

Example: Nape of neck to knee 41 in. x 2 = 82 in. + 4½ in. = 86½ in. (104 cm x 2 = 208 cm + 12 cm = 220 cm).

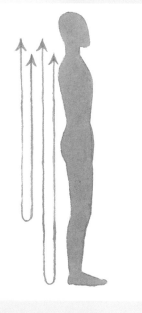

STEP 2 ▲ Fold the fabric in half lengthwise, right sides together, and cut the main piece 28 in. wide (71 cm) x half the length calculated above (so that it is the total length when opened out).

STEP 3
Calculate the length required for the neck/front bands as follows:
- Take the length from the nape of the neck to the hem, as before, plus 3 in. (8 cm) for the neck opening and 4½ in. (12 cm) for the seam allowance/hem turnings.

Example: Nape of neck to ankle
54 + 3 + 4½ in. = 61½ in.
(137 + 8 + 12 cm = 157 cm).
Cut two strips of the length required, 5 in. (13 cm) wide, on the straight grain.

STEP 4
Cut interfacing strips the same length but half the width of the neckbands.

STEPS TO SEW

Seam allowances of ⅝ in. (15 mm) are used throughout. Press at each stage before continuing to the next step.

STEP 8
▶ Using the folded length prepared earlier for the front and back, mark the center point along the fold line. Also mark shoulder points at either side along the fold line.

STEP 9
Working along the fold line, cut 3 in. (8 cm) on either side of the center mark to make a 6 in (15 cm) slit. Cut down the center front line to make the front opening.

STEP 10
For a man's small or a woman's medium to large kimono, make a tuck of ⅝ in. (15 mm) at the center back neck edge. For a woman's small version, make a 1 in. (25 mm) tuck. No tuck is needed for a man's medium or large size. Recut the 6 in. (15 cm) neck slit accordingly.

TIP: *Stay stitch the neck edge of the garment piece before sewing to prevent unwanted stretch.*

STEP 5
◀ Cut two sleeves 28 x 14 in. deep (71 x 36 cm). Shape following the diagram, so that the lower edge is 20 in. (51 cm).
(Traditionally, women's sleeves have curved lower edges and men's are angular. I chose the simpler male version to use here.)

STEP 6
Cut a tie, 5 in. wide x 72 in. long (13 x 183 cm), on the straight grain. Cut two loops, 4 x 1¼ in. (10 x 3 cm).

STEP 7
Cut two smaller ties, 12 x 1½ in. wide (30 x 4 cm).

STEP 11
▲ Fold the two front panels diagonally back toward the neck slit, as shown, and finger press. Leaving a ⅝ in. (15 mm) seam allowance, cut off excess.

STEP 12
◀ With right sides together, join the neckband pieces into one long strip. Apply interfacing to the wrong side of half of the strip.

STEP 13 ▶ Sew one edge of the neckband to the garment, right sides together, matching the center back tuck with the join seam in the neckband. Start at the center back and sew across the shoulder, turning sharply to sew down the front; then repeat for the other side. At the sharp neck angle, slit the fabric close to the seam, taking care not to cut the stitching.

STEP 14 ▶ With right sides together, pin the sleeve to the main fabric so that the shoulder point is at the center of the sleeve seam. Machine stitch together.

STEP 15 ◀ Starting at the hem edge of the sleeve, with right sides together, sew the back of the kimono to the front, along the sleeve and down the side seams, pivoting at the underarm point. Press. Clip seam allowances at the pivot point.

STEP 16 Press the raw edge of the facing to the wrong side ⅝ in. (15 mm) all around. Fold the facing only in half, right sides together, at the hem edge only and stitch through the folded facing only, 2½ in. (6 cm) from the bottom edge.

STEP 17 Turn to the right side, turning up all the hem edge of the garment at the same time. Press, tucking the raw edge of the hem under ⅝ in. (15 mm). Stitch in place.

STEP 18 ◀▼ Fold the neckband to the inside to encase raw edges and finish by top stitching or hand slip stitching.

FINISHING

STEP 19 ► Fold each tie piece lengthwise, right sides together, and stitch across one end and down the long edge to approximately the center. Reverse stitch to secure. Leave a turning gap and continue down the long edge and across the end. Snip corners at an angle. Turn through the gap, slip stitch the opening. Press.

STEP 20 ▼ Sew loop pieces as in Step 19, and press. Sew the ends together to form loops. Pin to the side seams at low waist height on either side, pinning the joined ends to the seam. Machine or hand stitch through all thicknesses.

► *Use a loop turner to pull the right side of the tie piece through the gap.*

STEP 21 ► Sew two small ties in the same way as in step 19. Press and stitch one end to the garment at a comfortable low waist height: one to the inside waist side seam, and the other to the front band edge at matching waist level.

TIP: *If making a reversible garment with fabrics of equal weight, cut both to the same measurements. A lighter fabric will probably need to be cut slightly bigger to accommodate the thicker fabric. Make a test piece by sewing two equal-sized pieces together along two sides. Turn through and check whether the unsewn sides still match up. If not, allow extra width on all pattern pieces.*

LINED/REVERSIBLE KIMONO (OPTIONAL)

1 For the lining, cut the garment section and sleeves only, using the same measurements as before.

2 Make the main garment as above, steps 1–8.

3 Stitch the lining sleeves to the lining body, as above, and press.

4 With the wrong side of the lining to the right side of the main fabric, pin and stitch the lining to the raw edge of the neck/front band. Start from the center back and stitch across the neck and down the front, as before. Repeat for the other side.

5 Trim the seam allowance, clip at curves, and turn through, folding the neck/front band in half. Press.

6 Finish as in steps 9–13 above. Stitch in the ditch between the front band and the garment edge to hold the lining in place (optional).

TROUBLESHOOTING

Occasionally, part of your sewing goes wrong or your machine doesn't work as it should. Many of these problems can be prevented or easily solved.

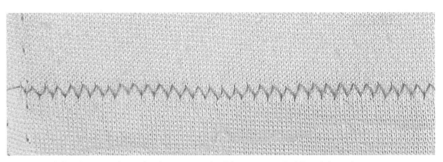

Fabric with broken stitching (top) compared with correct stitching (above)

Puckering caused by stitches that are too small

FABRIC PROBLEMS

Snagged fabrics The usual cause of snags is a blunt needle, or one with a slight burr. Change the needle. Snags can also be caused by using the wrong type of needle. A knitted fabric, which is stretchy, needs a ballpoint needle (it has a slightly rounded tip, which separates the fibers instead of piercing them). Fine silky fabrics need sharp-pointed needles. A full listing of recommended needles is included in Reference charts (page 124).

Puckered fabric This can be caused by stitches that are too small or too large. If the fabric puckers slightly as you stitch, the stitch length may be too short. Try lengthening it a little. If the fabric gathers as you stitch, the stitch length is too long, so shorten it to correct the problem.

Shading variations If there are variations in the fabric shading, it is because the nap is not always running in the same direction. Even fabrics with minimal nap can shade differently in natural light. If in doubt, always use the "with nap" layout to prevent uneven shading.

Sagging/stretching unevenly This problem can occur in fabrics that were cut off the grain line and therefore have more stretch in them, or in fabrics cut on the bias. Stay stitch (a line of regular stitching just within the seam allowance) areas that appear to stretch unnecessarily, such as shoulder seams, neck edges, and armholes. Leave bias-cut garments, such as skirts and dresses, on a well-padded hanger overnight to allow excess stretch to hang before hemming.

Puckering at interfaced areas This can be caused by iron-on interfacing that has not adhered properly. Always use a very hot iron and a press cloth, and apply with a pressing motion rather than ironing back and forth. Rest the iron for at least 10 seconds on the part of the garment that is covered with the press cloth, then lift and lower at the next position. Allow the fabric to cool completely before handling it again.

THREAD PROBLEMS

Threads keep breaking If the top thread keeps breaking, it is probably not running smoothly through the thread guides.
• Check that it is threaded properly.
• Check that it is unwinding evenly from the spool—it may be twisted around the spindle. This can happen if the spool moves up and down the spindle as you stitch. Add a spool (reel) cap (supplied with the machine) to keep the spool in place.
• Check that the spool is set the right way on the spindle. The thread should usually come over from the back to the front, but your sewing machine manual will show the correct direction for your type of machine.
• Do not use old thread, which can be weakened by age and break easily.
• Avoid using cheap thread, which can be uneven and prone to snap.
• A slight nick (invisible to the naked eye) in the eye of the needle can cause breaking thread. Nicks can result from the use of rough thread, such as metallic thread. Use a specially designed or large-eyed needle with such threads and insert a new needle for all other threads.

STITCH PROBLEMS

Skipped stitches These can occur because the thread is too tight—it is not feeding evenly through the thread guides—or because of problems with the needle. Take the top thread out and rethread it, checking that it follows the thread guide direction and goes between the disks. If the problem persists, check the needle—bluntness can cause skipped stitches. Prevent this by using a new needle for each project. The other possible cause is that the needle was inserted incorrectly. The general rule is "flat to back": The flat part of the needle is placed to the back. Check your sewing machine manual first, however, to confirm that this is right for your model.

Breaking stitches These are often caused by using a straight stitch on a stretchy fabric—when the fabric is stretched, the thread snaps. Use polyester-covered cotton thread for greater stretchability, and sew seams with small zigzag stitches.

Loose stitches The stitch length is too long for the fabric being sewn. Decrease the length slightly, and try again.

Stitch holes appear with stitches
Change the needle to a finer one that will not make such large holes. Use fine needles with fine fabrics.

MACHINE JAMS

Removing lint You should remove lint from the sewing machine after every project, and more frequently when sewing with fluffy fabrics, such as woolens, fleece, and knits. Take out the bobbin, blow out the lint, and use the brush supplied in the accessories case.

Oiling Modern machines are self-lubricating, but older models can need oiling. Check your sewing machine manual and follow the guidelines. Always sew scrap fabric after oiling to prevent surplus oil from damaging a project.

Buttonhole jam Always reinforce the area to be stitched with interfacing to provide a good base for the concentrated stitching. Avoid stitching too close to the edge of the fabric—if the presser foot has insufficient fabric to grip, the fabric can be drawn down into the throat plate.

Foot pedal doesn't work Check that the pedal is pushed firmly into the machine—it can work loose if the machine is moved. If the problem persists, ask your machine dealer to check the wiring.

No power Check the plug and fuse. Make sure the wire is pushed firmly into the machine. Check that the bobbin-winding spindle is not engaged, preventing normal sewing. If the problem persists, contact your machine dealer and have the wiring checked.

Insert the needle correctly. The general rule is: "flat to back."

PATTERNS

Patterns come up too large This is a frequent complaint, which is often the result of the design and wearing ease built into the pattern design but not readily visible in the pattern illustration (see Fit and ease allowance, page 27). Check the finished garment measurements printed on the pattern envelope or tissue before sewing. Remember, coats are designed to fit over jackets and thus have up to 12 in. (30 cm) of extra ease.

REFERENCE CHARTS

MACHINE NEEDLES

Choose the appropriate needle for each fabric type. The weight of fabric, number of layers to be stitched, and stitch density determine the needle size.

NEEDLE TYPE	FABRIC
Universal/multipurpose	Woven fabrics, synthetics, knits. Good all-purpose needle
Ballpoint	Knits, double knits, fleece, stretch, ribbing, fake furs
Stretch	Two-way stretch fabrics, lingerie, swimwear, Lycra, elastic
Jeans	Heavyweight cottons, canvas, denim, tightly woven fabrics, faux suede, faux leathers
Sharps/microfiber	Silks, satins, voiles, fine fabrics, polyesters, microfiber fabrics
Leather	Leather, suede, plastic
Embroidery	Machine embroidery, sewing with special or metallic threads
Quilting	Multilayer, patchwork/quilting
Twin	Works two rows of parallel stitching at same time; use needle size appropriate for fabric

NEEDLE SIZES

AMERICAN	EUROPEAN	FABRIC WEIGHT
9	60	Fine, lightweight, chiffon, voiles
10	70	Lightweight, organza, silks
11	75	Lingerie, swimwear, fine cottons
12	80	General dressmaking: cottons, lightweight woolens, polyesters, velvets
14	90	Heavier woolens, wool crepes, coatings, fleece, upholstery cottons
16	100	Heavyweight coatings, dense denim, canvas, heavy brocade
18	110	Heavyweight fabrics, multilayers, upholstery
20	120	Very heavyweight

TIP: *You may need to buy more fabric if you are working with an unusual pattern, one-way design, or "with nap" fabric. Check with your retailer.*

FABRIC CONVERSION CHART

When your chosen material differs in width from that listed on the pattern envelope, use this fabric width conversion chart to determine the amount of fabric required.

USING THE CONVERSION CHART

If a pattern calls for 2 yd. of 36-in. wide fabric (185 cm of 90-cm), and your chosen fabric is 45 in. (115 cm) wide, look across the table from 2 yd. under the 36 in. column to the 45 in. column. The amount of fabric required at the different width is noted here (1⅝ yd. or 150 cm).

FABRIC WIDTHS

36-IN. WIDTH	(90-CM WIDTH)	45-IN. WIDTH	(115-CM WIDTH)	54-IN. WIDTH	(140-CM WIDTH)	60-IN. WIDTH	(150-CM WIDTH)
1¾ yd.	(160 cm)	1⅜ yd.	(130 cm)	1⅛ yd.	(105 cm)	1 yd.	(95 cm)
2 yd.	(185 cm)	1⅝ yd.	(150 cm)	1⅜ yd.	(130 cm)	1¼ yd.	(115 cm)
2¼ yd.	(210 cm)	1¾ yd.	(160 cm)	1½ yd.	(150 cm)	1⅜ yd.	(130 cm)
2½ yd.	(230 cm)	2⅛ yd.	(195 cm)	1¾ yd.	(160 cm)	1⅝ yd.	(150 cm)
2⅞ yd.	(265 cm)	2¼ yd.	(210 cm)	1⅞ yd.	(175 cm)	1¾ yd.	(160 cm)
3⅛ yd.	(290 cm)	2½ yd.	(230 cm)	2 yd.	(185 cm)	1⅞ yd.	(175 cm)
3⅜ yd.	(310 cm)	2¾ yd.	(255 cm)	2¼ yd.	(210 cm)	2 yd.	(185 cm)
3¾ yd.	(345 cm)	2⅞ yd.	(265 cm)	2⅜ yd.	(220 cm)	2¼ yd.	(210 cm)
4¼ yd.	(390 cm)	3⅛ yd.	(290 cm)	2⅝ yd.	(240 cm)	2⅜ yd.	(220 cm)
4½ yd.	(415 cm)	3⅜ yd.	(310 cm)	2¾ yd.	(255 cm)	2⅝ yd.	(240 cm)
4¾ yd.	(435 cm)	3⅝ yd.	(335 cm)	2⅞ yd.	(265 cm)	2¾ yd.	(255 cm)
5 yd.	(460 cm)	3⅞ yd.	(355 cm)	3⅛ yd.	(290 cm)	2⅞ yd.	(265 cm)

GLOSSARY

BASTING
Temporary stitching to hold fabric layers together, using long stitches. Can be done by hand or machine.

BATISTE
Lightweight cotton or cotton-blend fabric used for underlining or heirloom stitching.

BIAS CUT
Fabric that is cut on a diagonal, or at 45° to the selvages.

BOILED WOOL
A felted, knitted wool, which has the stretchability of a knit but is also warm; good for jackets.

BROCADE
A shiny fabric woven with at least two colors, so that the background and design detail alternate on either side. Often made of silk and used for evening wear.

CHENILLE
A soft, textural fabric with a raised surface. It unravels easily, so the edges must be serged or overcast.

CUTTING LAYOUT
The manufacturer's guide to laying pattern pieces on fabric in the most economical way and keeping pieces "on grain" or on fold lines, and so on. A number of layouts are provided for different fabric widths and pattern sizes.

DAMASK
A heavy duty cotton fabric used for tablecloths, for example. It has a self-colored design in shiny fibers on a matte background.

EYELET (BRODERIE ANGLAISE)
Cotton fabric with a cutout design embroidered in self-color. Can be used as edging and usually has white cotton as a base. Also popular for use as curtains, especially in a kitchen or child's room.

FOLD LINE
Used to describe the position of pattern pieces to be placed on folded fabric. The fabric is folded, right sides together, usually lengthwise so that the selvages are together. A directional arrow on the pattern tissue indicates how to place the piece on the folded fabric.

GRADING SEAM ALLOWANCES
A layering of the seam allowances used to reduce bulk in the seams. One allowance is trimmed to a scant 1/8 in. (3 mm) and the other to 1/4 in. (6 mm). Used especially where several seams meet, or where a collar or cuffs join the garment.

GRAIN LINE
The fabric grain is the direction of the woven fibers. Straight or lengthwise grain runs along the warp thread, parallel to the selvages. Crosswise grain runs along the weft, perpendicular to straight grain. Most dressmaking pattern pieces are cut on the lengthwise grain, which has minimal stretch.

HAND/HANDLE
The term used to describe how a fabric feels, drapes, folds, pleats, etc. For example, this may be crisp, soft, heavy, or stiff.

LINE DRAWINGS
The black-and-white sketches of garments found on pattern envelopes and in catalogs. Line drawings show design points, zipper placement, and other details not apparent in the photograph.

NAP
The shading that occurs on piled fabrics. Pile is the term for the raised fibers on fabrics such as velvets and furs. A "with nap" cutting layout is used for fabrics with a pile, one-way shading, or design. Patterns are placed so that the pile will run in the same direction on all corresponding pieces.

NOTCHES/BALANCE MARKS
Triangular markings on the pattern tissue used to match two corresponding pieces. They can be single, double, or triple, and have the same combination of notches on pieces to be joined. Always cut the notches outward to avoid unraveling in the seam allowance.

NOTIONS
The small items needed to complete a project, including trimmings, zippers, and interfacings, which are listed on printed patterns.

PLACEMENT LINES
The lines printed on pattern tissue, indicating where design details, such as pockets, welt flaps, and front plackets, should be placed.

RAYON
A synthetic fiber and the various fabrics made from it (see also viscose).

SELVAGE
The side edges of fabric. These are often bound more tightly than the fabric weave.

SERGER (OVERLOCKER)
A special sewing machine that stitches seams, trims edges, and overcasts raw edges in one step.

SILK
There are many types of silk fabric, each with a slightly different finish. Fabric names include charmeuse, chiffon, crepe de Chine, dupion, gazar, georgette, noil, organza, raw, sandwashed, shantung, Thai, and tussah.

STITCH IN THE DITCH
A line of stitching within a previously stitched seam. Used to hold facings, turned bias binding, or waistbands in place, the stitching is worked from the front of the project.

STROKING THE CAT
The method used to determine which way the fabric will curl. Run a finger along the cut fabric edge to feel whether fibers lie flat or stand proud.

VISCOSE
A synthetic fabric, known in full as viscose rayon. The terms viscose and rayon are often used interchangeably.

WELT
A pocket style, with a "lip" or bound edge. Welts can be difficult to make and are best avoided by beginners.

WOOL CHALLIS
A medium-weight woolen fabric with a slightly rough surface. It makes beautiful pant suits, jackets, skirts, and dresses.

WOOL CREPE
Wool that is woven with a twisted yarn to give a slightly knobbly appearance. It is wrinkle-resistant and can be lightweight or medium-weight. Satin-backed crepe is an alternative that is double-sided and can be used either way.

INDEX

WEB RESOURCES AND CREDITS

There are many interesting and useful sites relating to sewing on the internet. I've listed here some good sources of tips, patterns, fabrics, and notions.

GENERAL REFERENCE

www.sewing.org
Online sewing lessons suitable for beginner sewers through to advanced. The instructions are very clear and easy to follow.

www.sewingmall.com
Post a question at the "Sewing at Home Forum" and wait for an answer from a more experienced sewer. You can also read questions and answers posted by other visitors.

www.sewmommy.com
This site offers a "Sewing Tip Exchange," where visitors are invited to "take a sewing tip … leave a sewing tip."

www.whatsthebestsewmachine.com
A good reference site to visit before buying a new sewing machine, offering an unbiased guide to many different models.

PATTERNS, FABRICS, AND NOTIONS

www.denverfabrics.com
This site is packed with a huge selection of patterns, fabrics, and notions. It has a secure online ordering facility.

www.ericas.com
This is a terrific site, full of sewing notions, fabrics, free projects, and more! It offers secure online ordering.

www.fashionfabricsclub.com
A huge selection of fabrics, all at wholesale prices.

PATTERN COMPANIES

Some commercial sites supply patterns via online ordering; others allow you to view designs before you purchase from a store. The web sites listed below are all international sites with links to the company sites based in different countries.

www.kwiksew.com
Provides information about Kwik Sew patterns and dealers.

www.marfy.it
Sophisticated Italian patterns and their international retailers.

www.simplicity.com
Shows all the current patterns from Simplicity and New Look. Also offers specialist catalogs for home use.

www.thesewingplace.com
Lovely sewing patterns from independent designers.

www.voguepatterns.com
The pattern collections from McCalls, Butterick, and Vogue.

SEWING MACHINE COMPANIES

The following sites provide information from sewing machine manufacturers about their latest sewing machines and sergers. Some also offer sewing tips, free projects, and dealer information.

www.babylock.com/babylock.co.uk
www.berninausa.com/bernina.co.uk
www.brother.com/brother.co.uk
www.husqvarnaviking.com
www.janome.com
www.pfaff.com
www.singer.com

CREDITS

The author and Quarto would like to thank Charlie Gardiner, Amy Gardner, Ryan Harris, Charlotte Knight, Edward Knight, and Tattie Reatchlous for modeling finished projects. Thanks also to Simplicity patterns for all their help, to Husqvarna Viking for the loan of their sewing machines, to Janome for use of the serger, and to Güetermann (www.güetermann.com) and Vilene (Pellon; www.vilene@freudenberg.de) for thread and interfacing, respectively, used throughout the book. Fabrics and trimmings pictured in the book were supplied as follows:

Straight Stitching: Shot Cotton Handweave by Rowan Fabrics (www.knitrowan.com); **Kit Bag:** Broad Check by Rowan Fabrics; **Topstitching:** Bali Handpaint by Hoffman Fabrics (www.hoffmanfabrics.com); **Pillow Power:** Bali Handpaint as above; **Trimmings:** selection by British Trimmings (www.britishtrimmings.co.uk/www.conso.com); **Ballerina Skirt:** lacy ribbon and pink trimmings by British Trimmings; **Bias Binding:** New Basics by Kaleidoscope Fabrics; bias binding by Coats Crafts (www.coatscrafts.co.uk); **Wonder Cape:** Blue, New Basics, and Flame Red by Kaleidoscope Fabrics; Bali Handpaint as above; satin bias binding by Coats Crafts; **Bags of Style:** selection of trimmings by British Trimmings; **Hemming:** New Basics as above; **Summer Shorts:** New Basics as above; **Seam Finishes and Edges:** New Basics as above; **Dreamy Windows:** printed voile by Crowson Fabrics (www.crowsonfabrics.com); Crystal header tape by Rufflette (www.rufflette.com); **Piping:** Bali Handpaint as above; **Trimmed Tiebacks:** Bali Handpaint as above; piping and beaded trims by British Trimmings; **Zippers and Other Fasteners:** New Basics as above; **Get Sporty:** Coated fabric, piping, and handle webbing by Pennine Outdoor (www.pennineoutdoor.co.uk); **Appliqué:** Pebble Beach, Flower Lattice, and Alternate Strip by Rowan Fabrics; **Hats Off!:** crushed velvet by Fabric Land (www.fabricland.co.uk); **Waistbands, Collars, Cuffs, and Facings:** Bali Handpaint as above; **Kimono Comfort:** Bali Handpaint and Cobolt by Hoffman Fabrics.